BIG LEAGUE

Baseball

PUZZLERS

Dom Forker

Illustrated by
Sanford Hoffman

Sterling Publishing Co., Inc.   New York

Library of Congress Cataloging-in-Publication Data

Forker, Dom.
    Big League baseball puzzlers / Dom Forker ; illustrated by Sanford
  Hoffman.
       p.   cm.
   Includes index.
   ISBN 0-8069-7336-6
    1. Baseball—Rules—Miscellanea.   2. Baseball—United States—
  Rules—Miscellanea.   3. Baseball—Humor.   I. Title.
  GV877.F594   1991
  796.357'02'022—dc20   90-24038
                                                CIP

10 9 8 7 6 5 4

First paperback edition published in 1992 by
Sterling Publishing Company, Inc.
387 Park Avenue South, New York, N.Y. 10016
© 1991 by Dom Forker
Distributed in Canada by Sterling Publishing
% Canadian Manda Group, P.O. Box 920, Station U
Toronto, Ontario, Canada M8Z 5P9
Distributed in Great Britain and Europe by Cassell PLC
Villiers House, 41/47 Strand, London WC2N 5JE, England
Distributed in Australia by Capricorn Link Ltd.
P.O. Box 665, Lane Cove, NSW 2066
Manufactured in the United States of America

Sterling ISBN 0-8069-7336-6 Trade
         ISBN 0-8069-7337-4 Paper

Contents

Introduction

If you think you know baseball and you want to test yourself, this is just the book for you.

In the first section, entitled "Tough Decisions," you, the reader are faced with situations that umpires face every day. Players and managers often think they know the answers and many times they don't, which leads to rhubarbs on the field and expulsion from the game many times. In this section, a hypothetical situation is given first, and the decisions follow, with the rule that applies. Then an example from real life follows, so you can see how and when the rule was administered.

The second section, called "Unusual Situations," is a selection of odd plays, circumstances and field eccentricities that seldom enter into a game, and when they do, they cause consternation among players and fans.

The third section, "Baseball Humor," quotes the best jokes and tales from the extensive lore that surrounds the game. Often, baseball players and fans think something is funny and the rest of the world wonders why. See if you are endowed with baseball humor.

"Is it legal to blow a ball foul?"

1
Tough Decisions

The Wind-Blown Ball

Bert Haas of the 1940 Montreal Royals in the International League, Lenny Randle of the 1981 Seattle Mariners, and Kevin Seitzer of the 1987 Kansas City Royals each had one thing in common: they were third basemen who attempted to blow slow-rolling balls foul before they reached the third-base bag. Haas and Randle succeeded. Seitzer did not.

By the way, is the play a legal one?

*   *   *

Well, it was, but it isn't any more. The Haas play was ruled a foul ball. The Jersey City Giants didn't protest the play by Haas or the call by the umpire. Even if they had, there was no rule at the time to cover the play. Shortly therafter, however, league president Frank Shaughnessy made Haas's play an illegal one.

Larry McCoy, who was the home-plate umpire when Randle made his play, initially ruled the ball foul, but correctly reversed his call. Rule 2.00, OBSTRUCTION.

At Bat Or Not At Bat?

Is it possible to get an official at bat without actually getting at bat?

✵   ✵   ✵

Yes, it is. Rafael Ramirez of the 1989 Astros will attest to that. Houston manager Art Howe changed his usual batting order before the game one lazy summer afternoon. He switched Ramirez and Alex Trevino, but the respective players were unaware of the change in the lineup before the game began.

Trevino came to bat in Ramirez' scheduled spot and proceeded to get a base hit. But before the first pitch to Kevin Bass, the next hitter, the opposing team appealed, saying Trevino had batted out of turn.

First, the umpires ruled that it was a double play. They called Trevino out for batting out of turn, and they also called Bass out. After Howe argued the call, however, the umpires correctly changed their ruling. They said that Ramirez, who was supposed to bat, was out, and they said that Bass, the next hitter in the order, was the proper batter.

Trevino's hit was taken away from him, but he was not charged with an at bat. Ramirez, on the other hand, never got an at bat, but he was charged with one.

The Saving Win

Can a pitcher get a win and save in the same game? The baseball rule book doesn't cover the possibility.

A game between the Mets and the Reds, early in the 1986 season that ultimately went fourteen innings is an example. But let's backtrack first.

With the score tied in the bottom of the tenth inning, Pete Rose hit a single and gave way to pinch-runner Eric Davis, who promptly stole second and third base. Ray Knight, the Met third baseman, thought that Davis was over-aggressive in his slide into third base, though, and a fight between the two players, and others, followed. The net result of the fight was that Knight and Davis, in addition to pitcher Mario Soto of the Reds and outfielder Kevin Mitchell of the Mets, were ejected from the game. Darryl Strawberry of the Mets and coach Billy DeMars of the Reds had been ejected in an earlier and separate incident.

Manager Davey Johnson of the Mets didn't have anyone, except a pitcher, to replace Mitchell in the outfield, so he decided to alternate Jesse Orosco, who was pitching, and Roger McDowell, another pitcher, between the mound and the outfield. Each would pitch a full inning and then switch to the outfield for a full inning.

Well, in the top of the fourteenth inning, Ed Hearn of the Mets doubled and Orosco drew a walk from Red pitcher Carl Willis. Ted Power then came on in relief for Cincinnati and promptly threw a three-run homer to Howard Johnson.

McDowell, who had pitched the thirteenth inning, then stood to be the winning pitcher, and that's the way it turned out when Orosco retired the Reds without a score in the bottom of the fourteenth inning. But suppose, just suppose, Orosco had gotten in trouble in the fourteenth inning, and had to be relieved by McDowell. Then if McDowell had retired the Reds without their tying or winning the game, wouldn't he have technically saved his own win?

Generally a pitcher can get a win or a save, but not both.

"The ball, the ball, where oh where is the ball?"

Search and Seizure

The 1987 Yankees had Rickey Henderson on second base and Willie Randolph on first when the White Sox pitcher's sinkerball bounced in front of the plate, caromed off the catcher's equipment, and landed in the home-plate umpire's ball bag.

But no one with the exception of the umpire knew where the ball was. He knew that he had had one ball in his bag. Suddenly he had two. He also had a dilemma. Should he stop the action and award bases? Should he tell the catcher where the ball was and let him search for it? Even if he did, how would he know which ball was the original one? How would you handle his dilemma?

✳   ✳   ✳

When this play occurred, there was no rule to cover the situation. But the home-plate umpire appropriately referred to Rule 9.01 c: Each umpire has the authority to rule on any point that is not specifically covered by the rules. The umpire in this instance stopped the action and advanced Henderson to third base and Randolph to second base, which, in his opinion, was where they would have gotten had the ball not landed in his ball bag.

Today, if the ball lodges in the umpire's or the catcher's equipment, it is a dead ball, and all runners are awarded one base. Rule 5.09 g and 7.05 i.

Shutout in Relief

Is it possible for a relief pitcher to hurl a shutout?

✳   ✳   ✳

Yes, it is. Rule 10.19 f—No pitcher shall be credited with pitching a shutout unless he pitches the complete game, or unless he enters the game with none out before the opposing team has scored in the first inning, puts out the side without a run scoring and pitches all the rest of the game.

✳   ✳   ✳

Babe Ruth of the 1917 Red Sox gave way to relief pitcher Ernie Shore under similar-type circumstances. Ruth walked the Washington Senator lead-off batter, Ray Morgan. When Ruth blasphemously objected to the umpire's fourth-ball call, he was ejected from the game. Shore replaced Ruth, Morgan was thrown out on an attempted steal, and the Red Sox relief pitcher proceeded to retire twenty-six batters in a row.

In essence, Shore recorded not only a shutout, but also the third perfect game in the history of modern-day baseball.

The Right of Appeal

Billy Martin was a player who tried to turn negatives into positives. In a game in the mid-1950s, he checked his swing on an oh-two pitch that bounced back to the screen.

Thinking that he might have broken the plane of the plate with his bat, he ran to first base, but was brought back to the batter's box by the home-plate umpire, who called the pitch a ball. Martin, not willing to give up a possible advantage too easily, appealed the call to the first-base umpire.

Does the first-base umpire rule or pass on the appeal?

✳   ✳   ✳

He must pass. Only the defensive team may request an appeal. Rule 2.00—An *appeal* is the act of a fielder in claiming violation by the offensive team. The ball call stands.

Ripken's Streak

Cal Ripken has played in all of the Baltimore Oriole games in each of the past eight years. Presently, he is closing in on Lou Gehrig's all-time record of 2,130 consecutive games.

Let us say that somewhere in his immediate baseball future, Ripken makes solely a pinch-running appearance in a game. Would that appearance extend his streak?

✳   ✳   ✳

No, it would not. Rule 10.24 c—A pinch-running appearance only shall not extend the streak. On the other hand, a consecutive-game playing streak shall be extended if the player plays one-half inning on defense, or if he completes a time at bat by reaching base or being put out. In addition, if a player is ejected from a game by the umpire before he can comply with the requirements of this rule, his streak shall continue.

Gehrig, by the way, extended his streak several times by either playing one-half inning on defense or completing a time at bat.

"No, no. Let him leap for the ball!"

Spectator Interference

The Oakland A's are losing by one run with two out and no one on base in the bottom of the ninth inning. Mark McGwire of the A's then hits a deep fly ball that clears the left fielder's reach and leaves the park for an apparent game-tying home run. But the left fielder claims that a spectator interfered with his making the catch.

What does the umpire do?

✳　　✳　　✳

If the umpire saw the hindrance, he should rule the batter out for spectator interference and impose other suitable penalties. In this case, the A's could not win since there were no runners on base. McGwire would be declared out and the game would end with the A's losing by one run. Rule 3.16, APPROVED RULING.

✳   ✳   ✳

In a real situation in the early 1960s, pinch-hitter Mickey Mantle of the Yankees was the batter, and Jackie Brandt of the Orioles was the left fielder. Mantle hit a dramatic home run that tied the game. Brandt argued that a fan had interfered with him. According to Brandt, he went back to the three-foot fence at Yankee Stadium and measured his leap to catch the ball. But the spectator, who was shielded from the umpires' view by the Oriole outfielder's body, slipped his hand around the back of Brandt's belt, and prevented his leap for the ball.

The umpires didn't see the spectator interference, however, and had to allow the game-tying blow to stand. The Yankees then won the game in extra innings.

The Forward Move

The Minnesota Twins pitcher, who is standing on the rubber, is getting his sign from his catcher when the Kansas City runner on third prematurely breaks toward home plate.

The Twins hurler, who has not yet started his wind-up, breaks directly toward the Royal runner and tags him before he reaches home plate.

Is the runner out? Suppose the pitcher had stepped back off the rubber before he chased and tagged the runner?

✳   ✳   ✳

When the pitcher leaves the mound without backing off the rubber, it is a balk, and the runner is awarded home plate. If he first backs off the rubber, it is a legal play, and the runner is out. Rule 801 (a, b, c) and 805 a.

In a 1976 game at Shea Stadium, pitching to the Dodgers' Ron Cey, the Mets' Craig Swan committed such a balk.

Error of Judgment

Dave Winfield, the Yankees' right fielder, has a strong arm. An accurate one, too. But once in a while an opposing runner will challenge his throwing prowess. Such was the case in the summer of 1986 when a Kansas City Royal speedster tried to go from first to third on a hard-hit single to right field. Winfield's throw was "right on the money," but it hit the sliding runner and bounced down the left-field foul line, allowing the runner to score.

Did Winfield receive an error on the play?

✶   ✶   ✶

Yes, he did. A tough one, by the way. He was penalized for making an accurate throw. But if he hadn't been assessed with an error, the pitcher would have been charged with an earned run. Rule 10.13 (e) NOTE The official scorer is caught in a double dilemma here. Some baseball purists think that in the above situation a team, rather than an individual, error should be ruled.

✶   ✶   ✶

One night at Yankee Stadium the author saw Al Kaline of the Tigers receive such an error. He made a great throw and ended up with the game-losing error. But sometimes a pitcher will make the "perfect pitch," and the batter will hit it for the game-winning home run. Is it a pitcher's error. These are some of the things which make baseball such an interesting game!

"Don't look now, but I forgot to touch the plate."

Return to the Scene of the Crime

The Yankees have a runner on second base with two out and Don Mattingly at bat. Mattingly singles to left field. George Brett, the Kansas City Royal third baseman, senses that the Yankee runner at second base is going to score easily, so he cuts off the outfielder's throw to the plate and fires it to second baseman Frank White, who tags out Mattingly, who is attempting to pick up an extra base on the expected throw. Mattingly is the third out.

In the meantime, the runner who "scored" misses tagging the plate, but there is no appeal. Should the home-plate umpire draw attention to the runner's missing the plate? Suppose the runner who "scored" later returns to the "scene of the crime" and touches home plate?

✳   ✳   ✳

The umpire should not draw attention to the runner's oversight. An appeal has to be requested by the defensive team. Rule 2.00 APPEAL.

In the late 1940s Joe DiMaggio once missed the plate on a play that was not followed by an out. But the Washington Senators, who were playing the Yankees that day, did not appeal the play, so the umpire said nothing, and DiMaggio stealthily returned to the plate to legally touch it.

In the case cited here, the umpire's decision is based on whether the runner touched the plate before or after the third out. Rule 4.09 a. Obviously he didn't touch at all, so if the defensive team appeals the play, the run doesn't count.

No Appeal

A Tiger base runner leaves third base early one day on a fly ball to Red Sox center fielder Ellis Burks, but Boston doesn't appeal the play.

Does the umpire make any call?

* * *

No appeal, no call. Rule 7.10 (a).

* * *

Stan Musial of the Cardinals did that one day. Richie Ashburn was in center field for the Phillies. Musial left third base before the ball touched Ashburn's glove. But Willie Jones, the Phillie third baseman, didn't call for an appeal. The run counted.

On the other hand, Smoky Burgess, who could hit but couldn't run, was notorious for leaving third base a split second too soon on a tag-up play. But opposing teams had a standard rule for Burgess—automatic appeal. And, more often than not, the run wouldn't count.

Caught Without the Ball

The Braves and the Phillies are scoreless in the seventh inning. Atlanta has Dale Murphy on third base with one out. On a ball that is hit back to the mound, he gets caught off third base, and a run-down ensues. As the Phillie third baseman and catcher exchange throws, the pitcher gets positioned in between the runner and the ball. Murphy, in trying to avoid being tagged out, runs over the pitcher.

Is there any call?

* * *

Yes, the runner is entitled to the advance base, in this case home plate. Rule 7.06 a.

* * *

This play happens every once in a while on a baseball field. For example, the visiting Indians and the Senators were scoreless in the eighth inning of a 1949 game. Eddie Robinson was the runner at third base. Early Wynn was the pitcher. As soon as contact was made, the umpire said to Robinson, "You score."

One of the intriguing things about that play is that Cleveland Indian manager Lou Boudreau was not aware that the obstruction rule existed, so he argued the call strenuously. The next day, he apologized to the umpires and told them they had made the right call.

Resumed Games

Resumed games can be tricky. Take the following Reds-Expos game in 1986.

Going into the sixth inning, the two teams were tied in a 1-1 game. But in the top of the sixth inning, Kurt Stillwell of the Reds singled home a run off Montreal's Tim Burke to give Cincinnati a 2–1 lead. Then rain, first, delayed the game and ultimately, suspended it.

Why didn't the Reds get a 2–1 win?

✳   ✳   ✳

In such a situation, when the visiting team goes ahead in the top half of the inning, the home team has to get its chance at bat, or the game has to be suspended and completed at a later date. Rule 4.11 (d-2). Since the Reds didn't have another scheduled game in Montreal, the game had to be finished in Cincinnati. On the surface that seems unfair to the Expos, but the Reds, playing in their own park, continued to be the visiting team. As the game turned out, Dave Parker of the Reds hit a grand-slam home run, and Cincinnati won anyway, 10–2.

"Who's supposed to be on this base anyway?"

The Step and Tag Play

Dave Winfield of the Yankees singles with one out in the top of the ninth inning. Don Mattingly, who follows him in the lineup, smacks a ringing line drive toward Blue Jay first baseman Willie Upshaw.

Winfield, thinking that the ball will be caught on the fly by Upshaw, retreats to first base, In fact, Upshaw fields the ball on a short hop, and Winfield, knowing that he cannot safely reach second base, remains on first base. Upshaw first steps on the bag and then tags Winfield.

Is it an inning-ending double play?

✴   ✴   ✴

No. Mattingly is out and Winfield is safe. As soon as Upshaw stepped on first base, he removed the force on Winfield. If Upshaw had tagged Winfield before touching the base, it would have been an inning-ending double play. Rule 7.08 e.

This play occurred in the top of the ninth inning of the seventh game of the 1960 World Series. Mickey Mantle of the Yankees was on first base, and Yogi Berra was the batter who hit the ball. Rocky Nelson of the Pirates was the first baseman. Asked afterwards why he didn't tag Mantle before he touched the base, he said, "They don't call me Rocky for nothing."

In the bottom of the ninth inning, Pirate Bill Mazeroski's game-winning, Series-winning home run made Nelson's choice academic.

The Crew Cut

A young Houston Astro pitcher with a crew cut constantly loses his cap during his wind-up.

Jim Bouton of the 1964 New York Yankees won two games in that year's World Series against the St. Louis Cardinals. In one of those games, his hat fell to the ground during his wind-up an unofficial thirty-nine times. All his pitches were legal. Rule 2.00.

The Tricky Tag-up

Rickey Henderson is the Oakland A's runner at third base. There is one out in the bottom of the ninth inning of a 3–3 game. Jose Canseco, the batter, hits a medium-distance fly ball to Red Sox left fielder Jim Rice. In the meantime, Henderson backs up several yards behind the third-base bag in order to get a running start by the time the ball is caught. Just as Rice catches the ball, Henderson hits the bag in full stride and goes on to score easily.

Do the A's win?

✶　　✶　　✶

Not if any of the Red Sox tag third base and make an appeal to the umpire who is assigned to that position. Rule 7.10 a—A running start is illegal on a tag-up play.

✶　　✶　　✶

Until the early 1950s Henderson's play used to be a legal one. But shortstop Alvin Dark of the New York Giants used the play to his and his team's advantage so often that the rules makers inserted 7.10 a and eliminated the loophole.

Gnatty Play

The 1946 Chicago Cubs have had games called under unusual circumstances. In a game against the host Dodgers at Ebbets Field, a swarm of gnats enveloped the field.

The day was sunny and the fans, who were annoyed with the gnats, tried to shoo them away with their white scorecards. The fluttering and flickering backdrop impaired the players' vision and endangered their safety, so the umpires called the game in the sixth inning.

Are games called under these or similar circumstances suspended, or are they handled like rainouts?

✶　　✶　　✶

The fog-out and the bug-out were both treated like rainouts. The Cub-Braves fogged-out game was cancelled because the tied game had not gone five complete innings. Rule 4.10 e. The Chicago-Brooklyn game reverted back to the last completed inning, so the Dodgers won, 2–0.

Today when a game is called, the score at the moment of termination is the final score, except when the visiting team has scored one or more runs to tie the game, or has scored one or more runs to take the lead, and the home team has not scored to tie or take the lead. Rule 4.11 d: 1–2.

The Blacked-Out Game

Umpire Harry Wendelstedt was behind the plate in New York when the lights suddenly went out in the sixth inning during the notorious three-day blackout in the Northeast some years back.

What's the umpire-in-chief's decision when he's standing in the dark?

*   *   *

The game is declared suspended and the action is resumed from that point. Rule 4.12 (a-3). The crew chief then documents the situation at the time of suspension. When the lights went out at Shea Stadium, there was a runner on first base. But when the game resumed at a later date, Wendelstedt noted that the runner had mysteriously advanced to third base.

"Oh no," Harry said, "we're not going to start that. You on third, first."

The players laughed. So did Wendelstedt. He didn't blame them for trying. Besides, he had the last laugh.

Temporary Ejections

Back in the early 1950s National League umpires had trouble with Brooklyn Dodgers "bench jockeys" who repeatedly questioned home-plate umpire ball-and-strike calls. Several times the plate umpire ejected all of the Dodgers on the bench who were not in the regular lineup that day.

In a case like this one, would the players be banished for the entire game?

*   *   *

Rule 4.08. PENALTY—In such a situation the umpire may clear the bench, but he must permit the dismissed players to return to the playing field for substitution, if needed.

*   *   *

Bill Sharman, the extraordinary basketball player, coach, and front-office executive, was one of those Dodgers players who was dismissed in a mass exit. Today he is also a footnote to the trivia of baseball history: he has been the only person who never played in a major-league baseball game who was thrown out of one.

Waiving the Rule

A recent Red Sox second baseman, in an attempt to distract a Minnesota Twins batter, positioned himself behind the pitcher and waved his arms frantically while jumping up and down.

Was his act a legal one?

* * *

It was until Eddie Stanky, the New York Giant second baseman of the early 1950s, employed the tactic one too many times. Because of complaints of his unsportsmanlike conduct, language 4.06 b was inserted in the rule book: No fielder shall take a position in the batter's line of vision, and with deliberate unsportsmanlike intent, act in a manner to distract the batter. The offender shall be removed from the game and shall leave the playing field.

* * *

The Red Sox second baseman was removed from the game.

"How silly can you get?"

Foggy Play

Many of us are familiar with the "Fog Bowl" between the visiting Philadelphia Eagles and the Chicago Bears at Soldiers Field during the 1988–89 National Football League playoffs. League officials temporarily considered calling the game because of fog, but ultimately permitted it to be concluded. The Bears went on to win.

A similar-type problem could—and has—occurred in baseball. Let us say that the present-day Brewers and the Tigers are threatened with a fog-out at Milwaukee's County Stadium. What criteria for calling off the game might the umpires employy?

✳   ✳   ✳

Visibility, of course, would be the key criterion. If the crew chief followed the precedent of umpire Frank Dascoli in a 1958 game between the Chicago Cubs and the Milwaukee Braves at County Stadium, he would take his crew into the outfield and have a modern-day Frank Thomas of the Cubs hit a fungo fly ball. If neither the four umpires nor the three outfielders could see the ball, he would declare the game fogged out.

Fielder's Choice

Kirby Puckett of the Twins, thinking of stealing second base, anticipates Milwaukee pitcher Juan Nieves's move and gets a good jump toward second. But Nieves throws to first base instead of second base. Puckett never breaks stride, however, and slides into second base safely as Milwaukee's first baseman throws the ball wildly into left field.

Does Puckett get a stolen base on the play?

✳   ✳   ✳

No, he does not. Rule 10.08 f. If he had made it safely to

second base without the aid of this error, or any high or wide throw, he would have gotten credit for a stolen base. Had he been thrown out, though, it would have counted as an attempted steal.

Darryl Strawberry of the Mets was picked off first base on such a play during the 1986 season. The Phillie first baseman, however, threw the ball away. Strawberry didn't get a stolen base. It was ruled an error on the first baseman and a fielder's choice.

Knockdown Pitch

Tony Armas of the Red Sox hits home runs the first two times he goes to the plate in a game against the Mariners. The third time up, on a two-oh count, he is hit with a pitch on the elbow by the Seattle southpaw. The home-plate umpire thinks that the Mariner pitcher hit Armas deliberately, and he also feels that the Seattle manager ordered the beanball.

What punitive power does the umpire possess?

✳   ✳   ✳

The umpire, when he thinks that the pitcher, on orders from his manager, hits a batter, he may remove both the hurler and the skipper from the game. Rule 8.02 (d-1).

✳   ✳   ✳

Jerry Koosman and manager Joe Torre of the Mets got ejected from a game for the above reason in 1978. Before 1978, when the new rule came into effect, it was more common for the pitcher to be fined and/or suspended.

One Off the Mound

Late in the 1986 season, the Yankees held a 5-4 lead over the visiting Indians in the bottom of the eighth inning. The Bombers had Rickey Henderson on second base and Don Mattingly on first base. Mike Easler was at the plate with two out.

Pitcher Frank Wills, on a two-two pitch, tried to throw the ball too fine and bounced a pitch in front of catcher Chris Bando. The Indian backstop blocked the ball, but it caromed off him toward the Yankee dugout. Henderson and Mattingly quickly moved up a base. But the Yankee television announcer got audibly excited, thinking that the Bombers would get possibly more runs if the ball went into the dugout.

Would they?

*　　*　　*

No. Runners can advance only one base on a pitch that goes out of play. Rule 7.05 h—APPROVED RULING. The same rule would apply if the ball had gone through a hole in the backstop or if it had become lodged in the mesh of the screen.

The High Strike Zone

Pete Rose of another day and Rickey Henderson of today batted out of an exaggerated crouch. Sometimes Henderson complains of high strike calls. Rose did, too. Why would umpires call a higher strike on Rose and Henderson than they would on other players?

*　　*　　*

Generally the feeling among many umpires is that the exaggerated crouch was not in Rose's case and is not in Henderson's case their natural stance. Henderson, as Rose did, rises up out of the crouch as the moundsman delivers his pitch to the plate. Rule 2.00, Strike Zone—Umpires must use their judgment on such calls. If this is not the player's normal stance and it is being used for trickery, the umpire should call a strike if the pitch is in what he judges to be the batter's normal strike zone, that is, the space over the plate between the batter's armpits and the top of his knees.

Who Gets the Putout?

The Padres in a game against the Giants have the bases loaded. Carmelo Martinez hits the first pitch to him to the fence in left field. The ball should be caught, but the left fielder for the Giants misplays the ball, it hits the base of the fence, and two runs score. But the Padre runner on first base, thinking that the ball would be caught, acts indecisively, and Martinez passes him on the base path between first and second.

Who is called out? Who gets the putout?

✳   ✳   ✳

Martinez is called out by the umpire for passing the runner. Rule 7.08 h. The fielder nearest the play gets credit for the put out. If the passing of the runner occurred closer to second base than to first, the second baseman would get the putout; if the passing took place closer to first base than to second, the first baseman would get it. Rule 10.10 (b–4).

✳   ✳   ✳

That play occurred in County Stadium, Milwaukee, in 1986. The Brewers, who were hosting the Yankees, loaded the bases in the bottom of the first inning. Robin Yount was on third base, Cecil Cooper on second base, and Gorman Thomas on first base. Ernie Riles then hit a ball to the base of the wall. It should have been caught, but it was misplayed by the Yankee outfielder, and it bounced off the base of the wall. Two runs scored. But an indecisive Thomas was passed between first and second base by the hard-running Riles.

Riles was called out by the umpire. The putout went to Willie Randolph, the Yankee second baseman.

"Do you think you can reach it?"

Ivy Time

Wrigley Field can present umpires with a unique set of problems. The outfield wall, as most people know, is covered with ivy, and it sometimes interferes with game play. Let's take the following two possibilities. One, suppose a batted ball gets stuck in the ivy? Two, suppose a batted ball grazes through the leaves of the ivy before the outfielder catches it?

What are the calls?

*   *   *

In the first situation, the batter is awarded a ground-rule double; in the second situation the outfielder has made a good catch. Rule 6.09 f and 7.05 f.

*   *   *

In another situation, Warren Cromartie of the Montreal Expos sprinted to the wall, leaped for the ball, which he deflected into the air, and caught it waist high on the way down. Herman Franks, the Cub manager, said that the ball on the way down had hit some leaves, so it should not be a legal catch. Umpire Andy Olsen disagreed, but added that there had been no solid deflection by the leaves. He ruled Cromartie's play a good catch.

Had there been a solid deflection—no catch. Ground-rule double.

Sacrifice Fly?

The Mets are in Cincinnati for a mid-season game in 1986. They have Wally Backman on third base and Keith Hernandez on first base with no out. Darryl Strawberry hits a slicing fly ball to the Reds left fielder. It is deep enough to score Backman from third base, but definitely a catchable ball. The fielder drops the ball, however, while Backman scores and Hernandez advances to second base on the play.

Does Strawbery get an RBI? Since the left fielder made an error on the play, is the sacrifice taken away from Strawberry, and does he get a time at bat instead?

✶   ✶   ✶

The official scorer gave Strawberry a sacrifice fly and RBI and didn't charge him with an at bat. The scorer reasoned that the hit, with less than two out, was far enough to score Backman, whether the fielder dropped the ball or not.

A Picky Play

A Seattle Mariners runner steals second base successfully, but in getting to his feet, he lifts his foot off the bag, and the Oakland A's second baseman applies the tag to him. Will the umpire call the runner out in this instance, or will he invoke the "neighborhood play?"

(The "neighborhood play" was made popular by Gil Hodges. If any first baseman or infielder had his foot in the neighborhood of the bag when he caught a throw, the umpire would consider it close enough, and it did not actually have to be in contact with the bag. In that way, it avoided a lot of injured toes and feet.)

✶   ✶   ✶

The umpire will call the runner out, but it will probably create a rhubarb. Rule 7.08 c. At least it did the day umpire Beans Reardon called Charlie Pick of the Cubs out on the play. First, Reardon called Pick out. Then, when the runner argued too vociferously about the call, the umpire threw him out of the game. Finally, when the Bruin outfielder responded too physically, Reardon "punched him out."

Errors and Earned Runs

Frank Tanana of the Angels gets off to an unlucky start. In the first inning he has runners on first and second bases with two out when Alan Trammell of the Tigers hits a catchable pop fly, in foul territory, to the California third baseman. But the fielder misjudges the ball, and it falls to the ground in foul territory untouched. Trammell, given a reprieve, proceeds to double both runners across home plate.

Do the runs count against the pitcher's earned run average?

* * *

Yes, they do. The third baseman, because he misjudged the ball and did not touch it, was not given an error on the play.

* * *

Lefty Steve Carlton of the Phillies struggled through the 1986 season. Third baseman Mike Schmidt didn't make Carlton's season any easier when he misjudged a pop fly under similar circumstances midway through the year. Because he misjudged the ball, he didn't get charged with an error. The next batter doubled two runs home. Carlton got charged with two tough earned runs.

Game-Winning RBI?

In Game Seven of the 1962 World Series, between the Yankees and the host Giants, New York's Ralph Terry out-pitched San Francisco's Jack Sanford, 1–0. In the sixth inning of that game, the Yankees loaded the bases with no out, and then Tony Kubek drove home the only run of the game when he grounded into a double play.

Did Kubek receive credit for a game-winning RBI?

*　　*　　*

No. Rule 10.04 b—Do not credit a run batted in when the batter hits into a force double play or a reverse force double play. NOTE: There does not have to be a game-winning RBI in every game.

Successful Steal?

In a game at Veterans' Stadium in Philadelphia, the Cardinals had Ozzie Smith on second base and Gene Tenace on first base with two out, when the Redbirds attempted a double steal. Catcher Bob Boone of the Phillies, realizing that he had no play on Smith at third base, threw to shortstop Larry Bowa to retire the follow-up runner at second base.

Did Smith receive credit for a steal?

*　　*　　*

No, he did not. Rule 10.08 d—When a double or triple steal is attempted and one runner is thrown out before reaching and holding the base he is attempting to steal, no other runner shall be credited with a stolen base.

"What's that behind me?"

The Assisted Home Run

The Tigers are playing the Orioles in a July game. Detroit's Darrell Evans hits a long fly ball to left-center field. The Oriole center fielder drifts back with the ball and appears to catch it easily as he backs into the fence. Upon the player's contact with the fence the ball pops out of his glove and bounces over the fence.

Is Evans' hit a double or a home run?

✶   ✶   ✶

It's a home run. Rule 6.09 h. The ball is considered to be

Tough Decisions   ✶   35

"in flight." Any ball in flight that leaves the park in fair territory is ruled a home run. If it had bounded off any physical structure of the park, such as the fence, instead of a player's glove, before clearing the playing field fence, it would be ruled a double.

✳   ✳   ✳

The above play occurred in an actual game on July 24, 1986, in a contest between the White Sox and the Orioles. Greg Walker of the White Sox hit the ball. Freddie Lynn lost it. Home run.

Who Can Sit on the Bench?

Two questions. One, can a player who is on the disabled list sit on his team's bench during an official game and two, can such a player, once he is granted permission, be requested to leave the bench during a game?

✳   ✳   ✳

The answer to both questions is "yes," but the opposing manager in one, has to give the permission and in two, has to make the request.

✳   ✳   ✳

This bizarre combination of compliances occurred some years ago in the National League. Frank Lucchesi, manager of the Phillies at the time, made the request of Gene Mauch, skipper of the Expos. Lucchesi wanted Dick Selma, an injured Phillies pitcher, to stay on his bench. Mauch gave his consent.

But Selma didn't like Mauch, so he loudly criticized Gene's every move during the game, so that Mauch could hear. In the sixth inning Mauch had had enough. He came out of his dugout and said to the umpire, "Selma has to go. I can't take him anymore."

Exit Selma. Rule 3.06.

The Good-Hitting Pitcher

Tommy Byrne, a good-hitting pitcher in the 1950s, used to pinch-hit periodically. One day he pinch-hit for Phil Rizzuto, his Yankee teammate who was batting eighth in the lineup. Then in the next half inning of the game he entered the contest as a relief pitcher. Billy Hunter substituted for Rizzuto in the lineup.

By the way, where would Byrne and Hunter bat in the lineup?

✳   ✳   ✳

Byrne would bat in the eighth spot and Hunter would hit in the pitcher's position. Rule 3.03 and 4.04.

Balk or Pickoff?

Dave Righetti of the Yankees is the pitcher in relief, and Rickey Henderson of the A's is the runner on first base. Righetti throws five consecutive pick-off attempts to first baseman Don Mattingly. In the meantime, Henderson extends his lead and finally Righetti, standing on the rubber in the set position, snaps a pick-off throw to Mattingly without stepping toward first base. Mattingly tags Henderson out.

Balk or pickoff?

✳   ✳   ✳

Rule 8.01 c—The pitcher must step toward first base ahead of the throw. Balk. Henderson is awarded second base.

✳   ✳   ✳

In reality, Righetti has a good snap pick-off move to first base. But he first steps back off the rubber with his pivot foot, thereby becoming an infielder, and he makes the throw with impunity.

Out of Position?

The National League places its second-base umpire inside the bag, that is, on the edge of the infield grass, when there is a runner on first base, a runner on second base, or runners on all three bases. Otherwise, the Senior Circuit arbiter positions himself behind second base. The American League places its second-base umpire behind the bag on all plays, that is, on the edge of the outfield grass.

What are the respective merits of each placement?

✳ ✳ ✳

National League umpires, most baseball people agree, are in the better position to call the steal and the force play. American League umpires, most baseball people concur, are in the better position to call the trapped ball in the outfield.

(Im)Perfect Play

When the field conditions are poor, the play is likely to be shoddy, too. Right?

✳ ✳ ✳

Not necessarily.

✳ ✳ ✳

Umpire Joe Paparella kept a game between the Yankees and host Orioles, on September 20, 1958, going despite bad field conditions, because Baltimore had a good crowd, and he knew that the Birds could use the money. That was the day Hoyt Wilhelm pitched a 1-0 no-hitter against the Yankees. By the way, that's the last no-hitter that's been pitched against the Bombers. On the other hand, Don Larsen of the Yankees allowed just one hit in the six innings that he worked as a starting pitcher that day.

It was the best game that Paparella had ever worked, and it probably shouldn't have been played.

"Hey, that was my elbow!"

The Hot Corner

One afternoon in the late 1940s Joe DiMaggio hit a hard smash down the third-base line that caromed off the arm of Detroit third baseman George Kell into the stands behind the visitors' dugout.

How many bases was DiMaggio awarded?

✻ ✻ ✻

Two. Rule 7.05 f—He gets the same number of bases he would have gotten if a fair ball he had hit went through or under, or stuck in a fence, scoreboard, shrubbery, or vines.

Experimental Play

In an attempt to speed up games, the American League in 1911 experimented with a rule that prohibited pitchers from making warm-up pitches between innings.

During a game between the Red Sox and the Athletics, Boston moundsman Ed Karger snuck in a few warm-up tosses while his teammates were trotting out to their positions.

Stuffy McInnis, the Athletics' first baseman who was on deck at the time, took advantage of the situation. He sneaked into the batter's box and smashed one of Karger's pitches off the fence in left field. McInnis then rounded the bases with an inside-the-park home run.

Did it count?

✱   ✱   ✱

Under the rules of the time, the umpires concluded, the play was a legal one. It was Karger who got penalized for an "illegal" attempt.

The Left-Handed Apology

The Seattle pitcher who is working against Boston has a reputation of doctoring up the baseball. In the second inning of a contest between the two clubs, the home-plate umpire becomes convinced that the Mariner hurler has been throwing either a spitball or a greaseball.

Instead of searching the pitcher under suspicion, though, the umpire arbitrarily disallows a swinging third strike, claiming that the delivery was an illegal one, and gives the batter another chance to swing.

Can the umpire do that?

✱   ✱   ✱

No, he can't, at least not according to Warren Giles, the former president of the National League. He took home-plate umpire Chris Pelekoudas to task for such a call. Pelekoudas made the call against Phil Regan, who was pitching for the Cubs at the time. Pete Rose of the Reds became the recipient of the extra swing.

Giles told Pelekoudas that the umpire was accusing Regan "a fine Christian gentleman" of cheating without clear evidence.

Pelekoudas ultimately had to apologize to Regan. Rule 8.02 (b-PENALTY-e).

Breaking the Tie

In a game between Los Angeles and host Cincinnati, the Dodgers second baseman is called out at first base on a bang-bang play. But the Dodgers contend that there was a tie between the runner's foot hitting the bag and the fielder's throw hitting the first baseman's glove. "Tie goes to the runner," they say. The umpire agrees there was a tie, but disagrees with their interpretation of the rule. He calls the runner out.

Who is right?

✳   ✳   ✳

The umpire is right. Some rule books do say that a "tie goes to the runner." But not the major-league rule book. There's no mention of a tie, in fact. The runner either beats the throw or he doesn't. In this case, he didn't.

✳   ✳   ✳

Steve Sax of the Dodgers was thus "victimized" in a real game. The play happens just about every day of the year on a big-league diamond.

Two Balls in Play

In a 1959 game between the Cardinals and Cubs, Chicago pitcher Bob Anderson walked St. Louis batter Stan Musial. But the Bruin catcher argued with home-plate umpire Vic Delmore that Musial had fouled off the three-one pitch, which was then rolling to the backstop. When Musial noticed that the ball was not being retrieved by the catcher, he sprinted to second base.

In the meantime, third baseman Alvin Dark tracked down the loose ball and fired it to shortstop Ernie Banks, who was covering second base. During the preceding play umpire Delmore had unthinkingly given Anderson a new ball, and the pitcher, trying to throw out Musial at second base, sailed the throw into center field. Musial, who saw the ball rolling freely, decided to advance to third base, but Banks then tagged the runner out with the ball that Dark had thrown to him.

You've got two balls in play. What's the ruling?

✻　　✻　　✻

Base umpire Bill Jackowski ruled Musial out because he was tagged with the original ball. The incensed Cardinals immediately protested the game, but later they dropped their challenge when they went on to win the game, 4-1.

The Easy Way?

The Padres, in a game against the Expos, have the bases loaded and two out in the bottom of the sixth inning. Jack Clark is the batter with a three-two count. On the pay-off delivery by Pascual Perez, the runners break with the pitch. Clark swings and misses. But the catcher drops the ball. Seeing everyone running, he hurriedly picks up the ball and fires it to the first baseman, who drops the ball. All of the Padre runners are safe.

How could the Expos have averted that catastrophe?

* * *

A cardinal rule of baseball is, don't make a throw unless it's necessary. In this instance the catcher simply had to pick up the ball and step on the plate for the force play that would have ended the inning. Rule 6.09 b and 7.08 e.

* * *

The Phillies were victimized by this mental and physical error in 1986. An inexperienced Phillie catcher picked up the dropped third strike and threw the ball to first baseman Von Hayes, who proceeded to drop the throw. A run scored and the opposition still had the bases loaded with two out.

A Steal or Not a Steal?

Walter "Boom Boom" Beck of the Phillies, forgetting that he has a runner on second base, goes into his wind-up rather than the stretch.

Frenchy Bordagaray, the Cardinal runner, gets a good jump and reaches third base before Chick Hafey, the batter, pops the pitch up to the second baseman. Bordagaray, thinking that he had legally stolen third base, makes no effort to return to second base. The second baseman flips the ball to the shortstop, who is at the bag, for the double play.

Should the runner have tried to return to second base?

* * *

Yes, because otherwise he is out, even though he reached third before the ball was put in play. (Rule 7.10 a)

"What's this I see?"

Two Gloves?

Rick Dempsey, catcher for the Orioles, decides to experiment one night: he comes out to home plate at the start of the game with his regular catcher's mitt on his left hand and a fielder's glove in his back pocket. He thinks that if he has a play at the plate, he will have a better chance of making it with a fielder's glove than with his catcher's mitt.

The home-plate umpire, who has never seen this done before, asks Dempsey not to carry the extra glove until the arbiter can find a ruling on the situation.

Does the ruling permit Dempsey to carry the extra glove?

✳   ✳   ✳

The rule book does not completely cover the situation. It says, however, that there cannot be any equipment left lying on the field, either in fair or in foul territory. That's close enough, the umpires conclude. They tell Dempsey that he cannot use the extra glove.

*   *   *

Clay Dalrymple of the Orioles tested that rule one night in the 1960s against the White Sox. Dalrymple promised the umpire that he would not use the extra glove until a ruling that covered the play could be found, though.

The rule referring to the gloves left on the field implies the offensive team can't leave them. Out of necessity, though, the umpires concluded that the rule also suggested that the defensive team can't leave them, either.

Since that ruling, it's been one glove per player.

Hit Batsman not Walk

In a game between the Expos and the Reds, Montreal has Hubie Brooks on third base, two out, and Andres Galarraga at the plate with a full count.

Tom Browning, the Cincinnati pitcher, hits Galarraga with the next pitch, and the ball rolls back to the screen. Before catcher Bo Diaz can retrieve the ball, Brooks scores and Galarraga hustles safely to second base.

Is Brooks allowed to score and can Galarraga stretch out an extra base on the play?

*   *   *

No. Galarraga has been hit with a pitched ball. He has not walked. The ball is dead once it hits Galarraga and neither base runner can advance. Brooks is sent back to third base, Galarraga is returned to first base. Rule 5.09 a.

Eyes in the Back of His Head

Let's zero in on a particular play in which a National League umpire, standing in front of second base, isn't in position to make a call. Staring at the pitcher, who is standing off the area of the pitcher's mound, he doesn't see the Met shortstop setting up the opposing runner at second base with the hidden-ball trick. The shortstop successfully pulls off the deception and makes a valid tag, the umpire has his back to the play, but he wheels around after the fact and makes the right call.

The team that is at bat argues profusely, saying an umpire cannot call what he doesn't see.

Can he?

✳   ✳   ✳

Yes, he can. A game between the Braves and the Giants at the Polo Grounds bears it out. Connie Ryan, second baseman for the Braves, pulled the play on Whitey Lockman of the Giants, who was called out. New York manager Leo Durocher argued vociferously. The umpire countered, "Didn't I get the call right?"

"Yes," Durocher said, "but you didn't see it, so you can't call it."

The umpire defended himself by saying, "I've got eyes in the back of my head."

But in reality what had happened was that he had looked at third-base umpire Al Barlick, who flashed him the out signal, and he in turn flashed the out signal to Lockman. The second-base umpire called the play through the eyes of the third-base arbiter.

The Free Swinger

Gus Zernial of the Athletics was so strong that his teammates called him "Ozark Ike." One day an opposing pitcher bounced a two-strike curveball a foot in front of the plate. But Zernial was fooled by the pitch and swung at it. To almost everyone's surprise, however, he lifted the ball over the left-center-field fence for a home run. It was no surprise that the opposition contended that the swing was illegal and Zernial should be a strikeout victim.

What's your interpretation?

✷   ✷   ✷

It's a home run. Rule 2.00 a BALL—If the batter hits such a pitch, the ensuing action will be the same as if he hit the ball in flight.

Follow-up Scenario

Let's carry the preceding scenario a few steps further. Suppose (1) Zernial with two strikes on him had not swung and the ball bounced through the strike zone? Or (2) the ball bounced and struck Zernial? Or (3) Zernial swung and missed the bouncing ball?

✷   ✷   ✷

One, it would be a ball. Two, Zernial would be awarded first base. Three, the catcher's simply fielding the ball cleanly would not constitute an out. The batter must be tagged as on any dropped third strike, or he must be thrown out at first base (unless first base is occupied before two are out.) Rule 2.00, A BALL and 6.05 c.

Line Drive

In a game between the visiting Pirates and the Cardinals, Pittsburgh's Jose Lind hits a vicious line drive that tears third baseman Terry Pendleton's glove off and carries it down the left-field line. In the meantime, Lind runs the play out to second base.

The Cardinals say Pendleton should get credit for a legal catch. The Pirates say that Pendleton threw his glove at the ball, so Lind should get awarded three bases.

What do you think the third-base umpire says?

✻   ✻   ✻

The third-base umpire tells Lind to stay at second base. (Rule 7.05 c—Pendleton's glove came off either accidentally or by the force of Lind's drive.) If he thought Pendleton had deliberately thrown his glove at a fair ball, and hit it, he would award Lind three bases. But that was not the case here.

Arm Signals

Dummy Hoy was a deaf-and-dumb outfielder for seven teams around the turn of the Twentieth Century. He had a .288 lifetime batting average for fourteen major-league seasons, and he stole 597 career bases. He was also responsible for the umpires raising their arms on ball-and-strike calls. Hoy couldn't hear the call, so he would turn around and look at the plate umpire. In time, the umpires started flashing him arm signals. It caught on.

The Invisible Mark

Suppose a player such as Roger Maris or Henry Aaron is approaching a cherished home-run mark, and the record to be made is dependent on such a player hitting a ball over the fence and possibly into the stands. How can the respective leagues be assured that the ball being returned by the person who claims to possess it is authentic? After all, the ball will eventually end up in the Baseball Hall of Fame in Cooperstown, N.Y.

∗ ∗ ∗

The respective leagues do it by using "Henry Aaron balls." When Aaron passed seven hundred career home runs, the umpires began to mark balls in games which Aaron played with invisible ink, and placed them in a special bag. When Aaron came to the plate to hit, those balls were used.

Every time he hit a home run in his countdown towards Babe Ruth's record, at least ten spectators would claim that they had the official ball. But only one of the balls that the claimants presented was authentic.

2
Unusual Situations

Almost everyone on occasion loses track of a run that is scored. But usually not the official scorer! In the following case, the official scorer did lose track of a run that scored. But there were extenuating circumstances.

In a 1989 contest between the host Yankees and the Brewers, New York was leading Milwaukee 4–1 in the bottom of the eighth inning. The Yankees had Mike Pagliarulo on third base and Bob Geren on first base with one out when manager Dallas Green flashed the suicide squeeze sign to batter Wayne Tolleson. The batter bunted the ball in the air to Brewer pitcher Jay Aldrich, who threw the ball to first base to double off Geren. In the meantime, Pagliarulo crossed home plate before the third out of the inning was recorded at first base.

In this situation the Brewers could have recorded a "legal fourth out." In order to do so, however, they would have had to make an appeal at third base before every infielder, including the pitcher, in walking off the field, had crossed the foul lines into foul territory. Rule 7.10 d. But they didn't do it. So even though Pagliarulo had left third base too soon—and he didn't return to the base to retouch it—his run counted because the double play was not a force or reverse force twin-killing.

At the time, plate umpire Larry Barnett didn't give an explicit explanation to the official scorer, so the run wasn't posted—until after the game! Thirty thousand fans left the park thinking that the final score was 4–1. Many of them found out in the next day's newspapers that the official score was 5–1, and that unknowingly they had witnessed one of the most unusual plays in the history of the game.

Umpire Barnett said after the game, "I've been in this game *twenty-six* years, and I've never seen that play."

Manager Green went seven years further: "I've been in this game *thirty-three* years, and I've never seen that play."

Many of the plays in the section occur once every *twenty-six* or *thirty-three* years. Not all of these plays ever occurred, but are included in this section to demonstrate a rule of baseball that may apply to a situation that occurs today or tomorrow.

Double Jeopardy

The Minnesota Twins have Dan Gladden on second base as Gary Gaetti hits a high hopper between the Chicago White Sox third baseman and shortstop. The third baseman gloves the ball and tries to tag Gladden, advancing from second to third base, but he misses. Then, trying to throw out Gaetti at first base, he hurls the ball wildly into the home team's dugout.

Where do the umpires place Gladden and Gaetti?

✳   ✳   ✳

The runners are entitled to two bases from their position at the time of the throw, since the fielder first attempted another play. Gladden, at the time of the throw, had not yet reached third base, so he's entitled to both third base and home plate. Gaetti, at the time of the throw, had not yet reached first base, so he's entitled to both first and second base. Rule 7.05 g.

"Just the ball, please!"

Loose Bat

Dave Winfield of the Angels has been known to let the bat slip out of his hands after a hard swing. Suppose, in a game against the White Sox, he hits a ball to shortstop Ozzie Guillen and lets go of the bat in the infielder's direction. While Guillen is trying to avoid the flying missile, the ball rolls past him for a "base hit."

Is it a case of safe hit or safety first?

Rule 6.05 h—If a whole bat is thrown into fair territory and interferes with the defensive player attempting to make a play, interference shall be called, whether intentional or not. In this case, Winfield is out.

But, suppose Winfield broke his bat during contact with the ball, and the broken half of the bat hit Guillen, thereby preventing him from making the play.

Interference?

Rule 6.05 h—If a bat breaks and part of it is in fair territory and is hit by a batted ball or part of it hits a runner or fielder, play shall continue and no interference shall be called.

The Balk before the Balk

The Cleveland Indians have a runner on second base when the Detroit Tiger pitcher commits a balk. During the pitch, however, batter Cory Snyder hits a ground ball to the third baseman, who first bluffs the runner back to second base and then throws the ball late to first baseman Dave Bergman.

Is the balk nullified because the batter-runner was safe?

✳   ✳   ✳

No. Each runner, including the batter-runner, must advance in order to nullify a balk call. The umpire moves the runner to third and directs the batter to hit again. Rule 8.05, PENALTY.

The Muffed-Ball Call

Mike Greenwell of the Boston Red Sox, with two out and no one on base, pops up to the Milwaukee first baseman, who first bobbles the ball and then loses it in fair territory. When he loses the ball, it hits Greenwell on the fly, in foul territory, and then bounces off him, without hitting the ground, into the glove of second baseman Jim Gantner, who is backing up the play. Is Greenwell the third out of the inning?

✷   ✷   ✷

No. It is considered a fair ball, but no catch. The Brewer first baseman initially touched the ball over fair territory. Rule 2.00.—A CATCH . . . It is not a catch if a fielder touches a fly ball which then hits a member of the offensive team or an umpire and then is caught by another defensive player.

Steps/Forward and Backwards

An Oakland A's slugger hits the ball over the left-field fence, but in rounding the bases, he misses touching first base. Enroute to home plate, between second and third base, the first-base coach attracts his attention to the fact that he missed first base, and encourages him to return to touch the missed bag.

The batter-runner retouches second base, returns to and tags first base, and then continues his home-run trot around the bases.

Is this legal?

✷   ✷   ✷

No. The ball is dead when it leaves the park. When the ball is dead, a runner may not return to touch a missed base after he has touched the next base. When the ball becomes live, the defensive team should appeal the play. If the defensive team doesn't appeal the play, the run counts. Rule 7.02, 7.10 b-APPROVED RULING, 7.10 b, PLAY b.

The Shoestring Catch

The Mets have runners on first and second base with one out when Tim Teufel hits a short fly ball to right field. Both runners, thinking that the ball will fall safely to the ground, set out for their respective advance bases. But Andre Dawson of the Cubs makes a shoestring catch and throws the ball to first base for an inning-ending double play just after the runner at second base crosses home plate.

Then the Cubs realize that the run will count unless they appeal the play at second base. But they have crossed the foul line leading to their third-base dugout. They rush back onto the field, and second baseman Ryne Sandberg grabs the game ball and touches second base.

Does the run still count?

✻   ✻   ✻

The run counts since the Cubs left the field before they made the appeal. Rule 7.10 d, Paragraph beginning "Appeal Plays"—The defensive team is off the field when the pitcher and all infielders have left fair territory on their way to the bench.

Umpire's Interference?

A Blue Jay infielder drills a fastball off the right-center-field fence and is legging out an apparent triple. But he runs into an umpire who is stationed in the base path between second and third base. The Toronto player falls to the ground, gets up groggily, and stumbles into the third baseman's tag.

Is the runner entitled to third base?

✻   ✻   ✻

Rule 2.00–INTERFERENCE (c)—When a runner collides with an umpire, it doesn't constitute interference, and the ball remains in play.

The Blue Jay in the above situation is out. He is supposed to avoid hitting an umpire.

"I'm not going to drop the ball this time!"

Using Mask or Cap

Seattle has Harold Reynolds on second base with Alvin Davis at the plate in a game at Anaheim Stadium. Davis singles to center field, Reynolds rounds third base, and center fielder Devon White throws to the Angel catcher in an attempt to "gun down" Reynolds at the plate. When the catcher sees that Reynolds is going to score easily, and the ball takes a skip hop to his right, he stabs the open side of his mask at the ball, and catches it in the mask. Anything wrong with that?

✳   ✳   ✳

The California catcher made a *faux pas* here. The runner on first base gets three bases. That's right, he scores. A fielder cannot deliberately touch a ball with his cap, mask, or any part of his uniform detached from its proper place on his person. Rule 7.05 b.

If an outfielder deliberately touches a fly ball with his cap, the batter-runner is awarded a triple, and he has the option to try to score at his own risk.

Unintentional Interference

A Houston Astro runner takes a lead off first base as the batter hits a hard one-hopper to Atlanta Braves first baseman Gerald Perry.

The runner, thinking that Perry will remove the force play by first stepping on the base, makes a false start for second base, then reverses himself and slides back into first base. But Perry throws to second baseman Ron Gant for the force play, and the pivot man's return throw to Perry bounces off the sliding runner, allowing the batter-runner to reach first base safely.

A man who has already been forced out can't interference with a follow-up play. Can he?

✳   ✳   ✳

The unintentional interference is not illegal, so the batter-runner is safe. Rule 7.09 f—If the batter or runner continues to advance—forward or backward to a base—after he has been put out, he shall not by that act alone be considered as confusing, hindering, or impeding the fielders.

One or More?

Rickey Henderson, the runner at first base for the Oakland A's, gets a quick break toward second base during an attempted steal.

The pitcher, whose stride foot has already made his move toward the plate and has broken the plane of the rubber, throws off-balance and wildly to first base. As the ball rolls down the right-field line, in foul territory, the home-plate umpire signals a balk while Henderson circles the bases and scores.

Does the arbiter return Henderson to second base on the balk award, or does he allow the run?

✳   ✳   ✳

He permits Henderson to score. Rule 8.05 APPROVED RULING—In cases where pitchers balk and throw wildly, either to a base or home plate, a runner or runners may advance beyond the base to which they were entitled at their own risk.

The Two-Out Fly Ball

The Pirates have Barry Bonds on third base and Bobby Bonilla on first base with one out when Andy Van Slyke flies out deep to the right-center-field fence. Bonds scores easily after the catch, but Bonilla, thinking that the ball is going to fall safely for a hit, rounds second base before the catch is made. He retraces his steps but is thrown out before he reaches first base.

Does the run that Bonds scored count?

✳   ✳   ✳

The run counts. This is not a force play, although the runner must return to first base. Rule 4.09 a—In the above situation, all the runners can score, if possible.

Protected by Being on Base?

Dave Magadan of the Mets takes a walking lead off third base in foul territory. Kevin McReynolds hits a hard ground ball in the base runner's direction. Magadan instinctively retreats to the sanctuary of the base, but he is hit by the batted ball in front of the third baseman.

Does the possession of the base protect Magadan from liability to be put out?

✳   ✳   ✳

Rule 7.08 f—The base does not protect the runner when he is hit by a fair batted ball before it has passed an infielder. If Magadan had been in foul territory when he was hit by the ball, it would have been a foul ball, and he would have been safe. But he was hit by the ball in fair territory before it had passed an infielder, so he was out.

What's the Score?

The Yankees are winning 1–0 in the top of the eighth inning when Don Mattingly hits a grand-slam home run. Then a huge downpour of rain causes the umpire to end the game. Is the final score 1–0 or 5–0?

✳   ✳   ✳

It is 5–0. Mattingly gets to keep his four-run homer. The home run did not affect the outcome of the game. The rule reverting back to the prior inning was changed in 1980. If Mattingly's home run had changed the result and given the Yankees the lead, the game would have been suspended and replayed at a later date. And, if Mattingly's home run had been hit in the bottom half of the inning, the game would have been over, with the Yankees winning 5–0. Rule 4.11 d.

Unannounced Substitute

It has been said already that whenever a new player takes a defensive position without notifying the umpire, he becomes an unannounced substitute.

One afternoon in 1970, managers Earl Weaver of the Orioles and Billy Martin of the Tigers found a loophole in the rule, though.

Norm Cash, the first baseman for Detroit, broke the webbing of his glove, and went to the clubhouse to repair it. In infield practice before the start of the following inning, Gates Brown substituted for him at first base. That brought Weaver running out of the Oriole dugout, insisting that Brown had to remain in the game as an unannounced substitute. But umpire Bill Haller permitted Cash to return to his position, saying that what happened in this situation was not the intent of the rule.

In the Orioles' next at bats, catcher Rick Dempsey made the final out of the inning, and went to put on his gear, so Kenny Singleton, the designated-hitter, warmed up the Baltimore pitcher. Then Martin bolted out of the Tiger dugout, demanding, "Singleton's catching. He's an unannounced substitute. He's gotta catch."

The umpires didn't buy Martin's theory, but the following day an asterisk was added to the rules, noting that a designated-hitter may warm up the pitcher without entering the game in the regular catcher's place.

Batter's Interference

Paul Molitor of the Brewers is on third base with one out. The Oakland pitcher takes a slow wind-up, so the Milwaukee infielder decides to steal home. The batter takes the pitch but his subsequent move illegally screens the catcher off the play, allowing the runner to cross the plate.

Someone has got to be called out for interference. Who? Would it make any difference if there were two out?

✷　　✷　　✷

Rule 6.06 c and 7.08 g—With less than two out the runner is called out; with two out the batter is ruled out. Neither way is the run allowed. In this particular play Molitor would be called out.

Removing the Force

The California Angels have Wally Joyner at third base, Johnny Ray at first base, two out, and their number-four man in the lineup at the plate with a three-two count. The batter grounds to the shortstop, who juggles the ball, then tosses it to the second baseman too late to force the sliding Ray. But Ray, just slightly after Joyner crosses home plate, overslides the base and is tagged out by the second baseman. Does the run count?

✷　　✷　　✷

Yes. Rule 4.09 a and 7.08 e—Ray's touching second base removed the force play. After oversliding the base, he had to be tagged in order to be retired. Joyner's run counts.

The Suspended Speaker

The Minnesota Twins are losing by three runs in the bottom of the ninth inning when Kent Hrbek hits what appears to be a game-winning grand-slam home run. But the ball hits a speaker that is suspended from the ceiling of the Hubert H. Humphrey Metrodome, and it comes down in fair territory, where it is caught by Boston Red Sox right fielder Dwight Evans.

Is the hit an out, a ground-rule double, or a home run?

*   *   *

It is an out! Situations such as this one are governed by the home team's ground rules. A ball that hits either the roof or a speaker in fair territory at the Metrodome is in play. If the fielder catches the ball on the fly, the batter is out and the runners advance at their own risk.

A Heady Play

In the bottom of the ninth inning, with the score tied, Tommy Herr of the Phillies is on first base with no out. On a hit-and-run play, Von Hayes smacks the ball behind Herr, and the spheroid caroms off the runner's helmet, which had fallen to the ground, and rolls down the right-field line. Herr rounds the bases and scores the apparent winning run.

Does it count?

*   *   *

Yes. A batted ball that accidentally strikes a helmet remains in play. The umpire views the play as if the ball had never hit the helmet. Rule 6.05. Paragraph beginning: "In cases where."

"Off the wall is OK, but off the speaker isn't fair!"

Double Penalty

A Blue Jay runner is on third base with one out when Toronto puts on the squeeze play. The Indian first baseman steals the sign and charges home plate. He catches the pitch before it reaches home plate and applies the tag to the runner five feet up the third-base line.

Legal play?

✳   ✳   ✳

No. There is a double penalty on the defensive team: a balk and interference. The runner scores on the balk. The batter is awarded first base on the interference. Rule 6.08 c and 7.07. Both penalties are the result of the first baseman's illegal grab.

Four-Run Mistake

The White Sox have Carlton Fisk on third base, Don Pasqua on second base, and their designated-hitter on first base when Ozzie Guillen, with two out, hits an inside-the-park home run. The runner on first base misses touching second base, however, and the second baseman, upon the completion of the play, calls for the ball, touches second and appeals the play.

How many runs count?

✳   ✳   ✳

None. Rule 4.09 a, 7.08 e, and 10.06 b—The appeal becomes a simple force play. It nullifies all four runs. Also, a batter does not get a hit on a play that results in a force play. Guillen is charged with an at bat, but no hit is credited.

The Risky Advance

The Reds have Eric Davis on first base with no out. Bo Diaz, the batter, lifts a foul pop toward the Phillie dugout at third base.

Mike Schmidt, the third baseman, drifts with the pop-up and catches it on the playing field, but his momentum carries him into the dugout. Davis tags up and tries to advance to second base, but Schmidt, from the dugout, fires a strike to second baseman Tommy Herr, who applies the tag to Davis for the out.

Does the umpire-in-chief allow Davis the advance base because Schmidt carried the ball out of play, does he permit the Redleg runner to advance at his own risk, or does he send him back to first base?

✶   ✶   ✶

Davis advances at risk to himself. Players may enter the dugout to make a catch. Rule 5.10 f.

Tagged Out Legally

Frenchy Bordagaray of the depression-starved Dodgers was a good pinch-hitter but a poor base runner. Out of desperation his manager, Casey Stengel, told Bordagaray to stay put once he got on base. One day Frenchy *almost* followed Casey's advice. But he started to hum a song, and then he started to tap the base with his foot when, lo and behold, he got tagged out *in between taps.*

Ball Enters Dugout

The Tigers' Lou Whitaker is on first base when Alan Trammell smashes what appears to be a sure extra-base hit to left-center field. Whitaker rounds second and is headed toward third base when Indian left fielder Joe Carter makes a spectacular one-hand running catch. Whitaker retraces his steps and is approaching first base when the shortstop's relay throw gets away from the first baseman and rolls into the dugout.

Where does Whitaker finally wind up?

✳   ✳   ✳

Rule 7.05 g—Whitaker is placed at third base. He is considered to be on first base because that is the base he will and must retouch before legally advancing. Two bases are awarded when the ball goes into the dugout.

Fair Game

Jack Clark of the Giants, with no out in the bottom of the ninth inning of a tie game, doubles to left and advances to third base on a ground ball out to second base. The Mets, hoping to throw out the potential winning run at the plate, play both their infield and their outfield shallow. Kevin Mitchell then drives a solid smash past third baseman Howard Johnson. The ball strikes Clark, who is standing in fair territory, and caroms down the left-field line in foul territory. Clark proceeds to hobble home with the winning run.

Is he safe or out?

✳   ✳   ✳

Rule 7.08 f—Any runner is out when he is touched by a fair ball in fair territory *before* the ball has touched or passed an infielder, and no other infielder has made a play on the ball. Because Johnson was in front of Clark when the ball passed him, the runner is safe. The Giants win.

Whose Interference?

Pete Reiser, the Dodger runner at third base, sees an opportunity to steal home against the Boston Braves pitcher, who has an extremely slow delivery. But catcher Ernie Lombardi sees "Pistol Pete" break for home out of the corner of his eye, and moves up to catch the pitch and block the plate.

Billy Herman, Brooklyn batter, doesn't realize that Reiser is running, so he swings at the pitch and hits Lombardi. Did Lombardi interfere with Herman's swinging the bat? What does the home-plate umpire do with Reiser? Herman?

✶　　✶　　✶

Penalize Lombardi for catcher's interference. Reiser scores and Herman takes first base. Rule 6.08 c—The batter becomes a runner and is entitled to first base without liability to be put out when the catcher or any infielder interferes with him. Reiser scores because of rule 7.04 d: Each runner, other than the batter, may without liability to be put out, advance one base while he is trying to steal, if the batter is interfered with by the catcher or any other infielder.

Courtesy Runner

Joe Carter of the Indians doubles to open up the top half of the second inning, but he sprains his ankle on his slide into second base. The game with the Red Sox is for first place, though, so Carter wants to remain in the game. In order to do so, however, he knows that he will have to get his ankle wrapped. He requests a courtesy runner and the right to return to the game in the bottom half of the inning.

Can he do that?

✶　　✶　　✶

Up until 1950 he would have been able to do it. Now, once removed from the game, a player may not re-enter, no matter what the circumstances. Rule 3.03 and 3.04.

"Oh, am I at third base already?"

Holding His Bat High

Orlando Cepeda of the Giants, and four other major-league teams believed each bat had only one hit in it, so as soon as he got a hit with a bat, he would discard it.

Other players tend to be overly protective of their bats. They use pine tar on them, they hone them, and they bone them. One such player carried his protective attitude to an extreme a few years back. He hit a triple and carried his bat with him, sliding into third base with his bat held high in his right hand. He did this for two reasons: one, he didn't want his bat to pick up a spot when he dropped it, and two, he didn't want another player to use it.

But is it legal for a player to hold onto his bat while he's running out his hit?

*   *   *

The batter-runner in this instance is certainly eccentric, but his eccentricity is a legal act. Rule 9.01 c—There is no rule which prohibits the batter-runner from carrying a bat while running the bases, so long as it does not hinder, confuse, or impede the defense.

The Three-Base Foul Ball

Is it possible for a batter to get three bases on a foul ball?

*   *   *

Yes, it is. Rule 2.00, FAIR BALL. Consider the following situation: The White Sox batter dribbles a ball down the third-base line. The Red Sox catcher runs down the line, throws his glove at the ball and hits it. A ball is not fair or foul until it passes first or third base or it settles in foul territory. If a fielder throws his glove at a ball and hits it, the batter is awarded three bases.

*   *   *

Frank Howard once hit a *bunt triple*—on the fair side of the third-base line. The opposing third baseman was playing "Hondo" as usual five feet out on the outfield grass. The pitcher came over and almost fielded the ball, but it just got by him. In a state of frustration, he threw his glove at the rolling ball—and hit it. That's an automatic triple. One of the shortest in the history of the game!

Switching Positions

Ernie Banks, who played more than 1,000 games at both shortstop and first base during his major-league career, twists his knee one day while running the bases. His manager, Leo Durocher, doesn't want to remove his star slugger from the game, so he simply switches Banks from shortstop to first base, a less physically demanding position, and changes his first baseman to shortstop.

But the Cub manager appears to have made a slip: he has forgotten to announce the changes to the umpires.

Does it matter?

✻   ✻   ✻

It's an act of common courtesy for the manager who is making the changes to inform the umpire(s) of the switches in the defensive alignment. But players already in the lineup may change positions without informing the umpires. There is no penalty. Rule 3.08 (a–3) and Rule 3.08 b.

Two-Strike Bunt Foul

Tony Gwynn of the Padres is on first base, and he is off and running with the pitch when pitcher Ed Whitson bunts a two-strike pitch into the air and foul down the third-base line. Kevin Mitchell, the third baseman for the Giants, sees that the pop-up is a catchable ball.

Should he catch it or should he let it drop to the ground?

✻   ✻   ✻

He should catch the ball and double Gwynn off first base. Whitson, of course, is a strikeout victim as the result of having bunted foul with two strikes on him. Rule 7.08 d—But when a two-strike foul bunt is caught, the ball remains in play—just as on any other legal catch. The runner, therefore, can be retired before he retouches first base.

The Infield Fly

Billy and Cal Ripken are on first base and second base, respectively, when a teammate hits a pop fly to the infield with no out.

However, the shortstop loses the ball in the sun, and the ball bounces and hits Cal, who is standing on second base at the time. As soon as the batter hit the ball, he was called out by the umpire on the infield fly rule.

Is Cal Ripken also out? If the infield fly rule had not been declared would he be called out?

✳   ✳   ✳

Ripken is safe. Rule 7.08 f—EXCEPTION: If a runner is touching his base when the infield fly rule is invoked, he is not out, but the batter is out. If no infield fly rule is called, he is called out because he has to advance, since a force play is in effect.

Let's suppose the infield fly rule had not been called. But Cal Ripken, who thought it had been, remains at second base, while Billy Ripken, who knew that it hadn't been, and who saw that the ball was going to drop to the ground cleanly on fair territory, dashes towards second base.

The ball bounces on the infield, caroms off Cal, who is standing on second base, and then strikes Billy, who is approaching second. Double play?

✳   ✳   ✳

No. Only Cal is out. 7.08 f—PLAY: If two runners are touched by the same fair ball, only the first one is out, because the ball is instantly dead when it touches the first runner.

Let's add one more wrinkle. Suppose, once again, the infield fly rule had been called, and Billy Ripken, who had been running (again), had been touched by the ball.

Double play?

✳   ✳   ✳

Yes, finally. Rule 7.08 f—If a runner is touched by an infield fly, when he is not touching the base, both the batter and the runner touched by the ball are out.

Juggle Ball

Robin Yount of the Brewers is on third base with no out when Rob Deer hits a long fly ball to right field.

Mel Hall of the Yankees reaches for the ball, deflects it into the air, juggles it a few times, and finally catches it.

Yount tags up at third base and leaves the bag as soon as Hall touches the ball for the first time, and he trots home easily with the run. But the Yankees, claiming that Yount left third base too soon, appeal the play at third.

Do they get a second out?

✶   ✶   ✶

No, they don't. Rule 2.00, A CATCH—A runner may tag up and leave the bag the instant a defensive player touches the ball. A catch is legal if the ball is finally held by any fielder, even though juggled, or held by another fielder before it touches the ground.

Triple Play?

The Royals have the bases loaded with no out when the batter, with an oh-two count on him, decides to surprise the defense by dragging a bunt. However, he pops the ball up halfway to the mound.

The runners think that the pop-up is an Infield Fly, so they remain close to their respective bases. But the pitcher can't reach the ball, and the backspin on it brings it back to the catcher, who is standing on home plate. He picks the ball up, with his foot on the plate, and throws it to the third baseman, who fires it to the second baseman for an apparent triple play. Is it?

✶   ✶   ✶

Yes. Rule 2.00, Infield Fly and 7.08 e—An attempted bunt cannot be an Infield Fly.

The Defense Appeals

The Blue Jays have the bases loaded, two out, and a three-two count on the batter. The pay-off pitch by the Seattle Mariner hurler goes wild, and the ball rolls back to the screen. The catcher, retrieving the ball, fires it into left field in an attempt to throw out the runner at third base. All three runners score and the batter-runner trots safely into second base. Then the first baseman appeals that the batter-runner missed touching first base. The umpire upholds the appeal. Do the runs count?

✳   ✳   ✳

No. The runs don't count because the third out of the inning was made on the batter-runner at first base. Rule 4.09 a and 7.04 d–NOTE.

The Comebacker

With Ryne Sandberg of the Cubs on second base with one out, the next batter strikes out, and heads directly toward his dugout on the first-base side of the field. But the opposing catcher has dropped the pitch. Suddenly Sandberg bolts toward third base, and Angel pitcher Mike Witt, now with the ball back from the catcher, throws him out. When the Chicago batter-runner, who is about ten feet from his dugout, sees that Witt's throw is to third base, he turns and sprints toward first base.

In the meantime, the third baseman after tagging Sandberg, throws the ball high over the first baseman's head. By the time the ball is retrieved and returned to the infield by the right fielder, the Cub runner is standing on third base.

Do the umpires permit him to stay there?

✳   ✳   ✳

Yes. The entire play is legal. The key to the play is that the runner did not enter the dugout. Rule 7.08, APPROVED RULING.

Interference at the Plate

Mark McGwire of the Oakland A's is the batter. Rick Cerone, who likes to position himself close to the batter, is the catcher for the Boston Red Sox. McGwire takes a mighty cut at a Dennis "Oil Can" Boyd fastball, and hits the ball over the left-field fence for an apparent home run. But the home-plate umpire notices that McGwire's bat made contact with Cerone's glove before it connected with Boyd's pitch.

Does McGwire get only one base because of Cerone's interference, or does he get four bases?

✳   ✳   ✳

Four bases. Rule 6.08 c—The batter becomes a runner and is entitled to first base when the catcher or any other fielder interferes with him. If a play follows the interference, the manager of the team at bat may tell the plate umpire that he elects to decline the interference penalty and accept the play.

Traded

Eddie Lopat is pitching for the Yankees against the Orioles when the game is suspended because of darkness. Before the game can be resumed, Lopat is traded to Baltimore. Coincidentally, it is his turn to pitch when the suspended game is resumed, weeks later. Can Lopat pitch for a team that he pitched against in that very same game, and can he pitch against a team he hurled for in that very same contest?

✳   ✳   ✳

The answer to both questions is yes. Rule 4.12 d—A player who was not with the club when the game was suspended may be used as a substitute even if he has taken the place of a player no longer with the club who would not have been eligible because he had been removed from the lineup before the game was suspended.

"Push me back, fellas, PLEASE!"

Head-First Play

With the bases loaded and one out, Darryl Strawberry of the Mets slices a fly ball down the left-field line at Shea Stadium.

Jerome Walton of the Cubs races from deep left-center field to make a sensational catch, but his momentum forces him to fall head first into the stands.

Is it a dead ball? Can the Met runners advance at their own risk? Does Walton have to return to the playing field before he can make a subsequent play?

*   *   *

Rule 5.10 f, 7.04 c—The ball is dead when a fielder, after catching a fly ball, falls into the stands or dugout, but each runner is entitled to advance one base.

Missing One Man

The San Francisco Giants and the New York Mets are playing one of their typical twenty-plus-inning curfew beaters. The score is tied 8–8 in the top of the twenty-third inning.

The visiting Giants have a man on first base with one out when their number-four batter hits into a double play. The runner, trying to break up the double play, makes an aggressive slide into second base, and breaks his ankle. The "bad break" is compounded when the Giants can't provide a substitute to take his place at third base in the bottom half of the inning.

Are the Giants allowed to take the field with eight players, or do they have to forfeit the game to the Mets?

✲ ✲ ✲

They lose the game by forfeit. Rule 1.01—Baseball is a game between two teams of nine players each. Rule 4.17—A game shall be forfeited to the opposing team when a team is unable or refuses to place nine men on the field.

Three-Run *Triple* Single

The Indians have the bases loaded with two out when their clean-up batter hits a ball off the wall good for three bases. Running out his hit, however, he misses touching second base. The second baseman notices the runner's oversight, calls for the ball, and makes a successful appeal.

Since it's the third out, do the runs count?

✲ ✲ ✲

Rule 4.09 a, 7.02, 7.10 b—The third out on the appeal did not occur until after the three Indian runners had scored, so the runs count. The batter, however, winds up with only a single.

Tape-Measure Home Run

Mickey Mantle hit so many tape-measure home runs that not even he can remember all of them.

One afternoon at Sportsman's Park in St. Louis, he hit one almost out of the state of Missouri. There was a runner on second base and one out at the time. When Mantle hit the ball, the runner, who was approaching third base, glanced over his shoulder to see where the ball was going to land. In doing so, he missed touching third base en route to home plate.

The Browns appealed the play at third base, and the umpire called the runner who missed the base out. But what about Mantle? Did he have to return to second base? Or was he out for passing the last legally touched base?

✶   ✶   ✶

Mantle got credit for a home run. Rule 7.12—Unless two are out, the status of a following runner is not affected by a preceding runner's failure to touch or retouch a base.

To Be or Not to Be

A Milwaukee Brewer manager of recent years sent up a pinch-hitter in the sixth inning, then changed his mind when the player got into the batter's box, and replaced him with another pinch-hitter.

Later in the game he sent up to the plate the pinch-hitter he had replaced to substitute-swing again.

Could he do that?

✶   ✶   ✶

No, he couldn't. Even if the initial pinch-hitter was not announced the first time, he was considered to be in the game when he took his position in the batter's box. Rule 3.08 (a-2).

Attempted (?) Steals

Rickey Henderson is an aggressive base runner. That is one of the reasons that he stole a record 130 bases in 1982. It is also one of the reasons that he was thrown out attempting to steal a record 42 times in 1982. Anticipating the pitcher's move to the plate, Henderson likes to take a walking lead to the advance base.

Let's consider three possibilities. First, Rickey is picked off while trying to directly return to the base that he left. Is the out recorded as an attempted steal?

No.

Second, he is picked off but he eludes a rundown and slides safely into the advance base. Is he credited with a steal?

Yes.

Third, he is picked off and tagged out while trying to reach the advance base. Is the out recorded as an attempted steal?

Yes.

The second situation is covered by rule 10.08 c: When a runner, attempting to steal, or after being picked off a base, evades being put out in a rundown play, and advances to the next base without the aid of an error, credit the runner with a stolen base.

The third situation is covered by rule 10.08 h (2): A runner shall be charged with "caught stealing" if he is put out, or would have been put out by errorless play when he is picked off a base and tries to advance—any move toward the next base shall be considered an attempt to advance.

Inning-Ending Double Play?

The Pirates have the bases loaded, one out, and Mike La-Valliere at bat. He tops a ball in front of the plate, but the topspin on the ball reverses its path, and finally it comes to rest directly on top of home plate.

The Phillie catcher picks the ball *off* home plate and throws it to first baseman Ricky Jordan for what appears to be an inning-ending double play.

Is it?

* * *

Rule 2.00-TAG, 7.08 c—Since the catcher did not make a definite tag of home plate, and since he did not have his foot in contact with home plate when he picked up the ball, it cannot be a force out on the runner from third. So credit only the out at first base, allow the run to score and the other runners to advance on the second out.

Two-Run Triple?

The Twins have Kirby Puckett at third base, a runner at first base, and Gary Gaetti at bat with two out.

As the pitcher begins his wind-up, the umpire calls a balk, but the hurler releases the ball, and Gaetti hits a two-run triple. The second baseman notices, however, that the runner from first base misses touching second base, and he appeals the play. The umpire agrees and calls the runner out.

Does Puckett's run count?

* * *

No. Rule 8.05 PENALTY, APPROVED RULING—The balk was nullified when the batter hit safely and the two runners advanced at least one base. In this case, the runner who missed second base is nevertheless regarded to have advanced to second base. Also, the third out was made on a force play, so no runs score.

"Hey, the ball's stuck in my glove. Take the whole thing, it's legal!"

Ball in Glove

The Tiger batter hits a hard smash back at veteran Yankee pitcher Tommy John. John catches the ball but he can't extricate it from the webbing of his glove. In frustration he runs toward first base and finally tosses the glove with the ball in it to first baseman Don Mattingly, who steps on the bag before the batter-runner reaches it.

Is the Tiger batter-runner out?

✻   ✻   ✻

Since the tossing of the glove with the ball in it violated no rule, the Tiger batter-runner is out. Rule 6.05 j.

Double Occupancy

The Astros have runners on first and second base when Glenn Davis lines a single to left-center field. The runner at second base starts for third base, but he runs into the shortstop in the base path, falls down and then staggers to the sanctuary of third base. In the meantime, the runner at first base turns second base and coasts into third base without a play.

Two Astros occupy the same base. Pirate third baseman Bobby Bonilla tags the second runner. Is he out? What happens to the first runner?

✻   ✻   ✻

The lead runner scores and the subsequent runner remains at third base because of the shortstop's obstruction. Rule 7.06 b.

You Can't Go Home Again

With two out Chet Lemon of the Tigers triples with the bases loaded. But the runner on third misses touching home plate. After the runners from second and first base score, he goes back to home plate to retouch it. The catcher then calls for the ball and appeals the first runner's miss of home plate.

Should the umpire uphold the appeal?

✳   ✳   ✳

Yes. Rule 7.10 b—APPROVED RULING, 7.12—The runner cannot return to touch a base after succeeding runners have touched it. In this case it represents the third out, so no runs score.

On the Rebound

Jack Clark of the Padres smashes a line drive that hits the pitcher's rubber and rebounds toward home plate. Catcher Gary Carter of the Mets reaches over the plate into fair territory, catches the ball, and throws it to first baseman Keith Hernandez for the out.

Or is it a foul ball?

✳   ✳   ✳

Clark is out. Carter fielded the ball in fair territory, so the ball is in play. If he had fielded the ball in foul territory, it would have been a foul ball. Rule 2.00, A FAIR BALL—It is not the position of the catcher's feet or body that counts, but the position of the ball when it is touched.

Stealing Home

Rod Carew stole home a record-tying seven times in one season.

In this hypothetical situation he is on third base and teammate Harmon Killebrew is on first base. Carew gets a big lead, flashes the double-steal sign to Killebrew, and breaks for home on the pitcher's wind-up. He crosses the plate safely before the pitch hits him in the strike zone. Killebrew, in the meantime, misses Carew's sign, but advances to second base when the bounding ball bounces toward the first-base dugout.

Is Carew out for being hit with the pitch? Is the pitch a strike? Is Killebrew allowed to advance to second base?

*   *   *

Carew is safe since he touched home plate before he was hit with the pitch. The plate umpire calls the pitch a strike since it was in the strike zone. If there were two strikes on the batter before the pitch, the hitter would be called out. If there were two out before a two-strike pitch, the inning would be over, but the run would still count, because it scored before the out was called. In addition, Killebrew is allowed to remain at second base because of Rule 5.09 h: Runner(s) may advance if any legal pitch touches a runner trying to score.

No Grand Slam?

Rob Deer of the Milwaukee Brewers comes to the plate in the fifth inning with the bases loaded and two out. He hits a grand-slam home run over the left-center-field fence, but the runner who was on first base misses second base and is subsequently called out on appeal.

How many runs score? What kind of a hit does Deer get awarded?

✳   ✳   ✳

No runs score and Deer does not get credited with a hit. Rule 7.12—If, upon appeal, the preceding runner is the third out, no runners following him shall score. If such third out is the result of a force play, neither preceding nor following runners shall score.

Unannounced Pinch-hitter

Suppose a manager sends up a long-ball threat as a pinch-hitter in the bottom of the ninth inning of a tie game, and fails to notify the home-plate umpire of the substitution. Then the batter hits the first pitch over the fence for the apparent game-winning home run. But the opposing manager appeals the pinch-hit, saying that the substitute batted out of order since he never officially entered the game.

Is it a proper appeal?

✳   ✳   ✳

The game is over as the result of the home run. The batter did not hit out of order because he was a substitute. Batting out of order occurs when a player already in the game bats in the improper spot. Rule 3.08 a-2—If no announcement of a substitute is made, the substitute shall be considered as having entered the game when, if a batter, he takes his place in the batter's box.

The Umpire's Mask

The Dodgers have the bases loaded with two out and a three-two count on the batter, Willie Randolph. Kirk Gibson is on third base, Eddie Murray is on second, and Mike Scioscia is on first. On the pay-off pitch all three Dodger runners break with the delivery, Randolph swings at the pitch and misses, but the ball gets past the Phillie catcher, and it lodges in the umpire's mask. Before the catcher can extract the ball from the umpire's equipment, all three Dodger runners score, and Randolph races to third base.

Do the Dodgers really score three runs on this play. Suppose there had been less than two out at the time? Would that have affected the play?

*   *   *

First, only Gibson's run counts. The ball becomes dead as soon as it lodges in the umpire's mask. Randolph is awarded first base, and each runner advances one base. If the play had occurred with less than two out, Randolph would be automatically out, since first base was occupied at the time, but each runner would advance one base. Rule 5.09 g, 6.05 c, and 7.05 i.

"You fell down. So what? Get going now."

Slip in the Mud

The Orioles' Billy Ripken and Cal Ripken break from second and first base, respectively, as Mickey Tettleton hits an extra-base hit to the wall.

Both runners will normally score easily, but Billy slips in the mud halfway between third base and home plate. Cal comes up behind Billy, helps him to his feet, and without passing his brother, pushes him in the direction of home plate. The two of them cross home plate just before the relay throw reaches the catcher.

Legal play?

✳   ✳   ✳

Yes—there is no penalty in the above situation. Rule 7.09 i—When a runner helps a teammate, there is no penalty. If a coach physically helps a runner, however, there is a penalty.

Checked Calls

Don Mattingly of the Yankees is on third base with two out and a two-two count on Dave Winfield. Teddy Higuera of the Brewers breaks off a hard-breaking curve ball that bounces in the dirt. Winfield appears to check his swing as the ball eludes Milwaukee Brewer catcher B.J. Surhoff and bounces back to the screen. In fact, the home-plate umpire calls the pitch a ball.

On the play, however, an alert Mattingly scores. An equally alert Surhoff appeals Winfield's checked swing to the first-base umpire, who rules that Winfield had indeed swung at the pitch. Surhoff then tags Winfield for the third out.

Does Mattingly's run count?

✳   ✳   ✳

The run does not count. Rule 4.09 a, EXCEPTION—A run is not scored if the runner advances to home plate during a play in which the third out is made by the batter-runner before he reaches first base.

✳   ✳   ✳

Dave Winfield's checked-swing call reminds us of other conflicting calls.

Ron Northey of the Cardinals once got tagged out at home plate at the end of his home-run trot. He had thought the ball he had hit was a home run. With good reason. A base umpire had flashed him the home run sign. But another arbiter had called the ball "in play." The protest that followed was upheld, and the game was replayed from that point.

Gus Bell of the Pirates once let two Cardinal runners score because he had seen third-base umpire Babe Pinelli rule his catch the third out of the inning. However, he had not seen second-base umpire Bill Stewart rule his play a trapped ball. Stewart was closer to the play, so his call stood.

Umpire Al Barlick once ruled a diving attempt by Andy Pafko of the Braves a trapped ball. Pafko was so sure that he had caught the ball on the fly that he ran directly to Barlick to argue the play. In the meantime, Rocky Nelson of the Cardinals circled the bases with one of the strangest inside-the-park home runs in major-league history.

Entrapment?

The Cardinals have one out, Vince Coleman on third base, Willie McGee on first base, and a rookie who is trying to make the St. Louis ball club at the plate. Zane Smith is pitching in relief for the Braves.

The rookie hits a high fly ball to short right field where Dale Murphy, who has noted that the batter-runner has stopped running midway on his path from home plate to first base, lets the ball drop at his feet. He then picks up the ball and fires it to first baseman Gerald Perry, who first tags McGee, who is standing on first, and then steps on the bag.

One out? Double play? Entrapment? Suppose Coleman had tagged up at third base and scored before the third out was made?

✳   ✳   ✳

Double play. Rule 6.05 l—APPROVED RULING and 7.08 e. There was entrapment. But it was the rookie who entrapped himself. If he had run out the play, Murphy's deception wouldn't have worked.

Coleman's run would not count. A runner cannot score on a force double play that ends an inning. Also, he can't score when the batter-runner makes the third out of an inning at first base.

Instant Ejection

A Kansas City player who is still seething over two close plays on potential base hits that went against him earlier in the game hits a home run in the eighth inning and proceeds to give the umpire at first base a mouthful of abuse as he rounds the bag. The umpire immediately ejects the runner.

Is the batter-runner out of the game as of that moment or can he legally complete his home-run trip before he has to leave the premises?

✲ ✲ ✲

The Royal runner is allowed to complete the play. Then he must leave the playing field. Rule 9.01 d—If an umpire disqualifies a player while a play is in progress, the disqualification shall not take effect until no further action is possible in that play.

Live-Ball Emergency

Willie Randolph has been plagued by leg problems during the twilight years of his career. Let us say that the second baseman hits an apparent double to the left-center-field wall, but in running out his hit, he suffers a hamstring muscle pull between first and second base, and can't complete his route.

Can a pinch-runner complete Randolph's course?

✲ ✲ ✲

No. A pinch-runner can't be inserted because the ball is live. Rule 5.10 e-1 says that if an accident to a runner is such as to prevent him from proceeding to a base to which he is entitled, that is, an award of one or more bases, a substitute runner shall be allowed to complete the play. Randolph wasn't "entitled" to two bases on the play. If the hit had been a ground-rule double, he would have been.

A Chancy Play

The first baseman bobbles a hard-hit ground ball, and then, trying to retrieve the loose ball, is run over by the batter-runner in his legal path to the bag. Did the batter-runner interfere with the fielder?

✻　　✻　　✻

No. The fielder had a chance to field the ball before the physical contact was made. Rule 2.00–OBSTRUCTION and 7.09 l.

Consecutive Game Streak

On the night that Pete Rose's hitting streak of 44 consecutive games was broken, he went hitless in four official at bats against Atlanta Braves pitchers Larry McWilliams and Gene Garber. Suppose he had gone to the plate five official times that evening and had walked, reached first base on catcher's interference, sacrifice-bunted, hit a sacrifice fly, and been hit by a pitch.

Would his streak have remained intact? Why? Why not?

✻　　✻　　✻

Rose's streak would have ended. Rule 10.24 b—The streak shall terminate if the player has a sacrifice fly and no hit. A consecutive-game hitting streak shall not be terminated if all the player's plate appearances—one or more—result in a base on balls, hit batsman, defensive interference, or sacrifice bunt.

Catcher's Balk?

Vince Coleman of the Cardinals is in a steal situation in the late innings, and the Pirate catcher is preparing for the potential theft attempt. While the Pittsburgh pitcher is in the middle of his delivery, the backstop jumps out of the catcher's box so that he will be in a better position to throw out the runner. Coleman runs, the catcher throws him out, and the Cardinals complain. They contend that the backstop committed a catcher's balk. Are they right?

✷　　✷　　✷

No, they are not. Rule 4.03 a—The catcher may station himself directly in back of the plate. He may leave his position at any time to catch or make a play, except that when the batter is being given an intentional base on balls, the catcher must stand with both feet within the lines of the catcher's box until the ball leaves the pitcher's hand.

The Quick Hook

Casey Stengel, managing in the National League, often pinch-hit in the first inning. If he got the chance to go for the big inning early, he would.

Let us say that three runs have scored, the bases are loaded with two out and he pinch-hits for the pitcher in the top of the first inning.

Good move?

✷　　✷　　✷

No. The umpire can't permit the substitution. He has to make the pitcher hit. Rule 3.05 a—The pitcher named in the batting order handed the umpire-in-chief as provided in rule 4.01 shall pitch to the first batter until such batter is put out or reaches first base, unless the pitcher sustains an injury. In the American League, since the D.H. (Designated Hitter) rule passed, the pitcher never bats.

The Slip Pitch

Every once in a while a hurler will experience a slip pitch. For example, the pitcher, with no one on base, runs a three-two count on the batter before a pitch slips out of his hand and dribbles twenty-feet toward the plate. Has the pitcher walked the batter? If the pitcher does the same thing with a runner on third base, is it a balk? Does the runner at third base score?

✳   ✳   ✳

In the first example it is no pitch, no walk. A pitch with no one on base has to cross a foul line to be considered a pitch. Rule 8.01 d—With men on base the same "pitch" is a balk. The runner at third base scores.

A Hustling Mistake

The visiting Mets lead the Cards in the top half of the sixth inning, 4–0. New York has Rafael Santana on first base, one out, and pitcher Bob Ojeda at bat. It is a bunt situation for the Mets. But pitcher John Tudor gets Ojeda to pop the bunt up behind the plate. The Cardinal catcher springs after the ball and makes a diving effort to catch it, but it just eludes his outstretched glove. It would have been a great play if the catcher had caught the ball.

But would it have been a wise play?

✳   ✳   ✳

No. It was a case of good hustle but poor thinking. If the Redbird backstop had caught the ball, he would have been in poor position to throw out Santana, who would have tagged up at first base and advanced to second after the catch. The Cardinals were trying to take away the bunt from the Mets. But in this case the catch would have been as good as a bunt.

Legal Catch?

Bill Doran of the visiting Astros hits a high drifting foul pop near the home team's dugout. Cincinnati Red first baseman Todd Benzinger drifts with the ball, makes a one-hand catch, and then, in order to prevent falling, extends his arms to brace himself against the top of the dugout. In doing so, the ball pops out of his glove and bounces into the stands.

Legal catch?

✲ ✲ ✲

No. Rule 2.00, CATCH—If a fielder drops the ball as a result of contact with a wall or dugout, it is not a catch.

The "Smart" Runner

Let us say that the visiting Red Sox have the bases loaded with no one out in a game against the Rangers. Dwight Evans is on third base, Marty Barrett is on second base, and Wade Boggs is on first base when Mike Greenwell hits a hard ground ball right at the shortstop.

Barrett, realizing that the ball represents a tailor-made double play, deliberately lets the ball hit him, thinking that one out is better than the probable two.

You're the second-base umpire. What's your call?

✲ ✲ ✲

If you think that Barrett intentionally interfered with the ball, you call him out and you have to call out the batter-runner, Greenwell, too. Rule 7.09 g.

Ron Luciano, the umpire, once made that call against Texas Ranger shortstop Toby Harrah. A heated argument followed, but Luciano prevailed, of course.

Jackie Robinson, the shrewd second baseman for the Brooklyn Dodgers, got away with that play several times in his major-league career, too.

Umpire's Error

Occasionally an umpire will make a mistake on the field that should not happen. For example, John McSherry, a very good arbiter, once called an infield fly with runners at second and third base and one out. Of course, for the umpire to rightfully make the call, runners have to be either on all three bases or on first and second base when a batter hits a catchable infield fly with less than two out.

What had happened in this instance was that there had been runners at first and second base and one out when a pitch got by Met catcher Jerry Grote. The runners each moved up one base, thus removing an infield fly situation. McSherry had somehow lost track of the runners' respective positions, though. So, lo and behold, he made a premature and illegal out call in front of fifty thousand New York fans.

How did he get out of his predicament? Well, he prayed: "Please, God, don't let Buddy Harrelson drop this fly ball! C'mon, Buddy, atta-boy, Buddy!"

Fortunately, Harrelson caught the ball, so McSherry was left with a red face, but not a scarlet one.

Raising the Mound

Attempting to confuse the opposing pitching staff, the home team adds four inches in height to its pitching mound. Can the host team alter the height of the mound? Or is the height of the mound regulated by major-league rule?

✳   ✳   ✳

Before 1950, mounds could be as high as fifteen inches in height above the basic baseball diamond. They could also be lower, though. In 1950 the height was standardized at fifteen inches. In 1969 it was reduced to ten inches flat. Rule 1.04.

Lightning Strikes Twice

The host California Angels are winning, 5–4, with the Seattle Mariners batting in the top of the ninth inning. Suddenly light failure halts the game. Then just before the lights are repaired, a lightning storm leaves the field in unplayable condition.

Is the game suspended. Or is it a complete contest?

✳   ✳   ✳

In this situation, weather takes precedence. It is a complete game. The Angels win, 5–4. Rule 4.11 d and 4.12 b–NOTE.

The Big Wind-Up

Nolan Ryan of the Texas Rangers, with a large lead in the ninth inning, takes a big, slow wind-up with Tony Fernandez of the Toronto Blue Jays on first base. By the time Ryan releases the pitch, Fernandez rounds second base.

In the meantime, batter George Bell hits a ground ball to the Ranger shortstop, whose errant throw winds up in the stands behind first base.

Does Fernandez score or stop at third base?

*　　*　　*

When Fernandez broke for second base, Ryan was on the rubber in pitching position, so Tony is considered to have been on first base when the play began. Consequently, he is only entitled to third base, and Bell is motioned to second base. Rule 7.05 g.

Getting the Drop on Him

The Mets have a runner on first base and one out in a game against the Cubs. Tim Teufel then lines a drive right at the Cub third baseman, who deliberately drops the ball, picks it up and throws to second baseman Ryne Sandberg, who pivots and fires to first baseman Mark Grace for an inning-ending double play. Does the play stand as the Cub third baseman designed it?

*　　*　　*

No. The rules protect the runner from this vulnerable situation. Rule 6.05 l—The batter is declared out, the ball is dead, and the runner(s) may not advance.

"That ball's not going to get away from me!"

Three Bases Only?

Von Hayes of the Phillies hits a line drive between the Astros' right and center fielders. In frustration the right fielder throws his glove at the ball and nicks it before it rolls to the wall. Hayes, circling the bases, tries for an inside-the-park home run. But the relay from center fielder Gerald Young to second baseman Bill Doran to catcher Alan Ashby nips Hayes at the plate.

Phillie manager Nick Leyva argues, however, that Hayes should be entitled to return to third base because the thrown glove hit the ball. Is Leyva right?

✳   ✳   ✳

No. Because the thrown glove hit the ball, Hayes *was* entitled to three bases, but he tried for four bases. On such a play the ball remains in play, and the runner at risk to himself tried to score. Rule 7.05 c.

He Can't Return Again

The Red Sox have a runner on first base when Dwight Evans hits a long fly ball to left-center field. The runner, thinking that the ball will hit the wall, rounds second base, but then retreats quickly when Kansas City Royal left fielder Bo Jackson makes a sensational diving catch.

In his rush to return to first base, the runner misses touching second base. In the meantime, Jackson throws the ball to the shortstop, whose relay throw to first base goes into the dugout.

What happens to the runner?

✶　　✶　　✶

The runner, on the throw into the dugout, is entitled to third base. Once the ball is dead, however, he cannot return to touch a missed base after advancing to and touching a bag beyond the missed base. An appeal in this instance would be valid. As soon as the ball is put in play, the defensive team has the right of appeal. If it fails to do so, however, the runner remains at third base. Rule 7.02 and 7.05 g.

The Quick Pitch

Rickey Henderson takes a lot of time setting up in the batter's box before he is ready to hit. The California Angel right-hander, this one day, is a quick worker, and he doesn't like to lose his rhythm, so he throws a quick pitch to the surprised Henderson. The hurler hopes to accomplish two things with his quick pitch: first, he wants to get ahead in the count and second, he wants to send a message to Henderson to be ready to hit the next time he steps into the batter's box.

Does he succeed?

✶　　✶　　✶

No. Rule 2.00, ILLEGAL PITCH, A QUICK RETURN PITCH, 8.01 d —The batter should be granted reasonable time to assume his stance. The umpire should hold up his hand, signaling the pitcher not to deliver, until the batter is set. If the moundsman makes an illegal pitch with the bases unoccupied, it shall be called a ball. An illegal pitch when runners are on base is a balk.

The No Throw

Dennis Rasmussen of the San Diego Padres has a unique move to second base. Working from the stretch position, he lifts his lead leg straight up in the air, suspends it there briefly, and then spins clockwise and throws to second base. Once, when he was pitching with the Yankees, he picked off Gary Pettis of the Angels with such a move. Then in his next outing he made the same move towards a runner at second base, stepped towards the bag with his lead foot, but didn't throw the ball. He simply bluffed the runner back to the base.

Was that a balk?

✶   ✶   ✶

No. Rule 8.05 c—The pitcher is to step directly toward a base before throwing to that base, but he is not required to throw (except to first base only) because he steps.

Collision Course

Atlanta Braves left fielder Al Hall and center fielder Dion James are racing for a line drive that has been hit between them. Hall makes a sparkling one-hand grab of the ball, but Jones runs into his teammate, and the collision jars the ball loose from the left fielder's glove.

Is it a legal catch? Suppose the collision had jarred loose both Hall's glove and the ball, which remained in the mitt as it was lying on the ground?

✷   ✷   ✷

First, it is an incomplete catch and the ball remains in play. Rule 2.00, CATCH—There is no such thing as a momentarily-held ball. To be a legal catch, the fielder must have firm control of the ball. In either case, Hall didn't. The ball is still in play.

Double Interference

The San Francisco Giants have runners on second and third base with two out when the batter hits a high-hopper towards the hole between third base and shortstop. The Los Angeles Dodger third baseman cuts in front of the shortstop and just as he gloves the ball, the runner who had been on second base runs into the shortstop, who was in the base path. The third baseman then drops the ball and all runners reach their advance base safely.

Or do they?

✷   ✷   ✷

All runners are safe. The inning continues and the run counts. Only one fielder is entitled to the right of the interference rule. Since the third baseman actually fielded the ball, the runner's contact with the shortstop is incidental. Rule 7.09 l.

Batter's Request

In the bottom of the seventh inning, the Twins have Kent Hrbek on third base with two out. The batter, with an oh-two count, steps out of the batter's box while White Sox pitcher Britt Burns is delivering the next pitch. He does not request time out. Burns stops in the middle of his delivery. The umpire makes no call.

What is the call?

✳   ✳   ✳

No call. Rule 6.02 b—The batter shall not leave his position in the batter's box after the pitcher comes to Set Position, or starts his wind-up. If the pitcher pitches, the umpire shall call "Ball" or "Strike," as the case may be. If after the pitcher starts his wind-up or comes to a "set position" with a runner on, and he does not go through with the pitch because the batter has stepped out of the box, it shall not be called a balk. Both the batter and the pitcher have violated a rule, and the umpire shall call time, and both the batter and pitcher start over from "scratch."

Blocking the Plate

Tim Raines of the Expos is on second base when Hubie Brooks lines a single to center field. Raines tries to score on the play, but he slides into the Cincinnati Red catcher, three feet from home plate, before the ball skips by the receiver.

Pitcher Tom Browning, who was backing up the catcher on the throw from the outfield, retrieves the ball and throws it to first baseman Barry Larkin, who is covering the plate. He tags Raines before he can touch the plate. In the meantime, Brooks advances to second base.

Does the play stand?

* * *

No. Obstruction is called on the catcher for blocking the runner without possession of the ball. The run scores and the subsequent action is inconsequential since the ball is dead. Brooks is returned to first base. Rule 7.06 a.

After the Fact

The Orioles have runners on second and third base with two out when Mickey Tettleton hits a long fly ball to the outfield. The runner from third base tags up and scores easily, and the runner from second base tags up and advances to third base. But the second baseman for the Texas Rangers claims that the runner at second base left the bag too soon, and the umpire, upon appeal, agrees with him. The runner is called out.

* * *

Does the run count?

* * *

The run scored before the third out, so it counts, because the final out of the inning was not a force out. Rule 4.09 a.

Haste Makes Waste

The Pirates have runners on second and third with one out when Barry Bonds hits a medium-distance fly ball to Montreal Expo left fielder Tim Raines. The runner on third base, in his haste to score, leaves the bag before Raines makes the catch. On Raines's throw to the plate, however, the ball gets away from the Expo catcher, and both runners score.

The Pirates make an appeal on the first runner, who left third base early, and get the third out of the inning.

Does it nullify the follow-up runner's score?

✷   ✷   ✷

Yes. Since the play results in the third out, the appeal retires the side, and the run doesn't count. If it had resulted in the second, rather than the third, out, the follow-up runner would not be affected, and his run would count. (Rules 7.10 a and 7.12).

Shedding Some Light

Now that the Chicago Cubs have lights, baseball people at Wrigley Field have the opportunity to see both day and night baseball.

Let us say that the umpire-in-chief, during a rain-interrupted day game, orders the Cub technicians to turn on the lights in the bottom of the seventh inning. Met manager Davey Johnson protests to the crew chief, citing discrimination. He says that the lights, if they are to be turned on, should be done so at the start of an inning, so that one team does not have a distinct advantage over the other.

Is Johnson's protest a valid one?

✳   ✳   ✳

No, it is not upheld. Of course, the umpire-in-chief should follow common courtesy in this regard, but he may legally turn the lights on at any time. Rule 4.14—The umpire-in-chief shall order the playing field lights turned on whenever, in his opinion, darkness makes further play in daylight hazardous.

In Flight?

A lazy fly ball is hit to Phillie left fielder Bob Dernier, but it hits a bird in flight before the Phillie outfielder catches the ball.

Was the ball caught in flight?

✳   ✳   ✳

No. (Rule 2.00, Catch-In Flight—It is not a legal catch.) The ball remains in play, the batter is safe and can advance at his own risk.

Obstruction or Interference?

Lenny Dykstra of the Phillies, with runners on first and second base with no out, pops up a bunt between the pitcher's mound and the first-base line. The Padre pitcher dives in fair territory for the ball, deflects it into foul ground, and in the process rolls into Dykstra, who falls to the ground.

In the meantime, catcher Benito Santiago picks up the ball and throws it to the first baseman for the out.

Legal play?

✳ ✳ ✳

No. The umpire calls obstruction on the pitcher. As soon as the Padre moundsman bumps into Dykstra, without the ball in his hand, the ball is dead. Dykstra is awarded first base, and the other runners are awarded the bases to which the umpire thinks they would have advanced if there had not been any obstruction. (Rule 2.00—Obstruction and 7.06 a.) The Phillies have the bases loaded with no one out.

Whose Call?

An hour before a game between the Padres and the Cubs, heavy rain descends upon Wrigley Field in Chicago and saturates the playing field. Shortly before the game, as the respective managers bring their lineups to home plate, Cub skipper Don Zimmer informs the umpires that he is canceling the game.

Does he have that right? Suppose the game had already started when the heavy rains fell. Who would then have the authority to halt play permanently?

✳   ✳   ✳

The home-team manager, with two exceptions, has the authority to postpone the game before it starts. First, if the initial game of a doubleheader has been played, the umpire-in-chief of the first game decides if the second game should start. Second, in the last series of the season between any two clubs, the league president can undertake the authority, which he usually does by authorizing an umpire to make such a decision for him. Once the home-plate umpire receives the lineups from the respective managers, the decision to start or postpone a game lies solely with the umpire-in-chief. Rule 3.10 a-b.

Change of Mind

After a fourth ball gets past the catcher and goes to the backstop, Brett Butler, the batter-runner for the Giants, entertains the thought that he might be able to reach second base on the play.

Catcher Sandy Alomar of the Padres retrieves the ball quickly, however, and Butler changes his mind before he reaches first base. But he is running too fast to stop suddenly at the base, so he crosses it and runs approximately thirty feet down the right-field line. He returns to the base immediately, though.

Can first baseman Jack Clark tag Butler out before he returns to the base?

✳   ✳   ✳

No. (Rule 7.08 c–j, 7.10 c)—The rules don't treat a batter who has walked any differently than any other batter-runner. As a result, Butler has the same right to overrun first base.

No Kick Here

Von Hayes of the Philadelphia Phillies bunts the ball hard down the first-base line. The Atlanta Braves pitcher races over to the line to field the ball, but bobbles it, and deflects it into the base line. Then Hayes accidentally kicks the ball before reaching first base safely.

May he stay there?

✳   ✳   ✳

Yes. (Rule 7.09 m—If, in the judgment of the umpire, the runner (did not) deliberately and intentionally kick such a batted ball on which the infielder had missed a play, then the runner shall (not) be called out for interference.) In this case the kick was accidental, so Hayes is safe.

Mental Mistake

The Blue Jays have Tony Fernandez on third base, George Bell on second base, one out, and a three-two count on Fred McGriff, who strikes out on the pay-off pitch.

The Brewer catcher, thinking that there are three out, flips the ball to the umpire and walks toward the dugout. The umpire, momentarily confused, rolls the ball toward the mound while Fernandez and Bell both streak across the plate.

How does the home-plate umpire unravel the double mental mistake?

✳   ✳   ✳

Very simple. He credits both runs. The umpire's handling of the ball doesn't affect Fernandez' and Bell's scoring on the play. Rule 5.08—It is the same as if the umpire had been hit accidentally by a thrown ball. The ball remains in play.

The Umpire's Offensive Assist

Kevin Bass of the Astros hits a hard ground ball that strikes an umpire who is standing behind the mound. The ball bounces off the umpire to Phillie second baseman Tommy Herr, who throws out Bass at first base.

Is Bass really out?

✳   ✳   ✳

No. The ball is dead when it strikes the umpire under these circumstances. Bass receives credit for a single and is placed at first base. This is the ruling when a batted ball strikes an umpire in fair territory before touching a fielder. Rule 5.09 f and 6.08 d.

The Umpire's Defensive Assist

Suppose in the preceding scenario Bass's grounder got cleanly past the Phillie second baseman, hit the umpire behind the fielder, and then deflected to Herr, who threw out the runner at first base.

Would Bass be out then?

✳   ✳   ✳

Yes. If a batted ball strikes an umpire after it passes a fielder, other than the pitcher, it remains in play. Rule 6.08 d. Bass is out.

The Heady Runner

Kansas City has a runner on first base with one out when George Brett singles to right field. Dave Winfield of the Yankees, who has a very strong arm, charges the hit and throws the ball to third base, trying to cut down the advancing runner. En route, between second and third base, the runner is hit in the head with the ball, and he falls unconscious to the ground. Then the Royal third-base coach calls for a time out as Yankee shortstop Nino Espinoza picks up the free ball and tags the stricken runner.

Can Kansas City call for a time out in that situation? Can Espinoza apply a legal tag?

✳   ✳   ✳

Rule 5.10 h—The offensive team can request a time out, but it won't be granted by the umpires until all action on the play has ended. The runner is out.

Wrong Language

Salome Barojas of the White Sox was pitching one day with the bases loaded. Jim Fregosi, who was managing the Sox at that time, sent one of his coaches to the mound to speak to Barojas. When the coach got to the mound, however, he realized that he couldn't speak Spanish, so he signaled to the Spanish-speaking third baseman to come over to the mound to act as an interpreter.

That constituted a second visit to the mound during the same at bat. Barojas had to leave the game.

Back to the Mound

A pitcher must throw to at least one complete batter, or retire the side, before he may be removed from a game, right?

Home-plate umpire Greg Kosc had trouble with that rule during a 1989 game between the Twins and the Red Sox. The host Twins were defeating the Red Sox that night, and they had two runners on base with one out. At that point Minnesota manager Tom Kelly inserted left-handed-hitting Jim Dwyer to pinch-hit. Red Sox manager Joe Morgan countered by bringing in left-handed-pitcher Joe Price. Dwyer wanted to bunt the first pitch, but at the last moment he tried to check his swing. But Kosc called the pitch a strike, Dwyer argued the call vehemently, and the umpire ended up throwing him out of the game.

Kelly then sent right-handed-hitting Carmen Castillo up to the plate to take Dwyer's place, so Morgan naturally brought in a right-handed-pitcher, Mike Smithson, to face Castillo. After Smithson had completed throwing his warm-up pitches, Kelly informed the umpires that a pitcher has to face one complete spot in the batting order, regardless of how many players occupy that spot.

Crew chief umpire Barnett sent Smithson back to the bullpen and directed Price, who had been in the dugout, to return to the mound and conclude pitching to that spot in the lineup. Price proceeded to strike out Castillo.

The Four-Out Inning

The Padres have the bases loaded with two out when the batter singles between the third baseman and the shortstop into left field. Two runs score before the runner who had been at first base gets caught in a rundown between third base and second base, and is tagged for the third out of the inning.

Then Met first baseman Keith Hernandez says that the Padre batter-runner missed first base, calls for the ball, and successfully appeals the play.

Is it possible to record "four outs" in an inning? Do the two runs count?

✳   ✳   ✳

Yes, it is possible to record "four outs" in an inning. The above situation is an example. Since the batter-runner never legitimately advanced to first base, the runs are nullified. The appeal takes precedence if it develops during the same play in which the third out is made. Rule 7.10 b, Paragraph beginning "Appeal Plays."

The Overslide

Jim Rice of the Red Sox is up at the plate with the bases loaded, two out, and a full count. Dwight Evans is on third base, Mike Greenwell is on second base, and a rookie just up from Pawtucket is on first base.

The three players are off-and-running on Texas Ranger pitcher Nolan Ryan's delivery, which is a fourth ball that forces in a run. But the rookie runner going to second base slides and goes past the bag. Catcher Geno Petralli, seeing that the runner has overslid the base, alertly throws the ball to his second baseman, who makes the tag before the rookie can return to second base and before Evans crosses home plate.

Does the run count?

✳   ✳   ✳

It might seem contradictory, but permit the run and call the runner who overslide second base out. Rule 7.04 b— Each runner, other than the batter, may without liability to be put out, advance one base when the batter's advance without liability to be put out forces the runner to vacate his base. A runner forced to advance without liability to be put out, such as when a walk forces the advance, may advance past the base to which he is entitled only at his own peril. If such runner, forced to advance, is put out for the third out before a preceding runner also forced to advance, touches the plate, the run shall score.

Rookie Mistake

The Dodgers have Eddie Murray on third base and a rookie on first base with one out. Kirk Gibson hits a ball to the center-field wall but Dale Murphy makes a sensational catch, spearing the ball with his glove extended high above the fence. Murray scores easily on the "sacrifice fly." But the runner on first base, thinking that the ball is going to drop for at least two bases, rounds second base before he applies the brakes and retreats to first base. On his way back to first base, however, he neglects to retouch second base. Eventually he is called out via the appeal process.

Does Gibson get a run batted in? Does the run count?

✳   ✳   ✳

Yes. Gibson gets an RBI, a sacrifice fly, and no at bat. Also, Murray's run counts. Rule 4.09 a—A run is not scored if the runner advances to home base during a play in which the third out is made (1) by the batter-runner before he reaches first base; (2) by any runner being forced out; (3) by a preceding runner being declared out because he failed to touch one of the bases.

3
Humor in Baseball

Wrong Pitcher

Once in a while a manager will signal to the bull pen for one pitcher, but a different one will show up at the mound.

And it can happen to the best. One day in the late 1950s Yankee manager Casey Stengel thought that his starting pitcher, Whitey Ford, was getting tired, so he called the bull pen and asked for Johnny Kucks, a sinkerball pitcher, to come on in relief. But bull pen catcher Darrell Johnson, who answered the phone, thought Stengel said "Trucks" instead of "Kucks."

When (Virgil) Trucks showed up at the mound, Stengel almost fainted, but he regained his composure and didn't say anything. Only Ford and catcher Yogi Berra knew that Stengel had wanted Kucks. As it turned out, Trucks threw one pitch, a game-ending double play ball, and then Stengel expounded to the reporters for hours after the game the reason that he called on Trucks, rather than Kucks, in that critical situation.

Only Ford and Berra knew that Casey really wanted Kucks.

Drysdale Humor

Umpire Augie Donatelli once raced out to the mound and searched Dodger pitcher Don Drysdale, whom he suspected of throwing a spitball. First he checked Drysdale's hat, glove, and uniform. Finally he ran his fingers through Don's hair. When he was through with his futile search, Drysdale said, "Didn't you forget something?"

"What?" Donatelli asked.

"Usually when people run their fingers through my hair, they give me a kiss, too."

Not Joe DiMaggio

Some people claim that umpires give certain players the benefit of the doubt: Joe DiMaggio and Ted Williams, for example, Wade Boggs and Tony Gwynn, too.

Skeeter Newsome, an infielder for the Philadelphia Athletics, was at the plate one day when umpire Bill McGowan called him out on a close pitch after a three-two count. Newsome's pride was offended. "You wouldn't have called (Joe) DiMaggio out on that pitch," he said resentfully.

"You're darn right I wouldn't," McGowan shot back. "He would have hit it off that 457-foot sign in left-center field."

No-Play

The most exciting play that took place in a game between the 1989 Mets and Giants was a no-play.

Ernie Riles of the Giants was on first base and Kirt Manwaring was the batter with two out. Randy Myers, the relief pitcher for the Mets, stretched, checked the runner, and threw to the plate. Riles broke on the pitch, Manwaring swung at the offering and missed, and catcher Barry Lyons, trying to throw out Riles at second base, threw the ball into center field.

Riles bounced up from his slide and bolted towards third base. Seeing the third-base coach waving him home, he rounded third and raced to home plate. In the meantime, center fielder Lenny Dykstra picked up the errant throw and fired a strike to catcher Lyons, who tagged the sliding Riles for the *fourth* out of the inning.

Manwaring's swinging strike was the third out of the inning. But Riles, Lyons, Dykstra, and home-plate umpire Jerry Layne lost track of the number of outs. Sheepishly, Riles said afterwards that he was practicing his base running, Lyons claimed he was practicing his throws to second base, Dykstra contended he was practicing his throws to home plate, and Layne asserted he was practicing his out call.

Walter's Fastball

When Walter Johnson of the Washington Senators was in his prime, one of his fastballs broke his catcher's hand in the middle innings of a game. Umpire Billy Evans, who was more than a little bit concerned about his own health behind the plate, beseeched the substitute catcher, "For God's sake, protect me, will you?"

Johnson's first pitch to his new catcher bounced off Evans' leg. His next pitch hit Evans on his chest protector. "That's all," Evans wisely proclaimed, tongue in cheek. "Game's called on account of darkness."

Was It a Strike?

Richie Ashburn complained about a strike call to home-plate umpire Jocko Conlan one night.

"Okay," Jocko said, "I'll let you umpire and hit at the same time."

Ashburn was initially reluctant, but he finally agreed. "Okay," he said.

The next pitch was two inches inside. Ashburn hesitated in his call of the pitch, and then finally said, "Strike."

"Strike!" Conlan half yelled and questioned at the same time. Then he took off his cap and dusted the plate. Finally he said to Ashburn, "You had the first and only chance in history to hit and umpire at the same time, and you blew it. No more. I'm not going to let you give umpiring a bad name. From now on you're just a hitter."

Roasting the Umpire

Figuring out who are the strident bench jockeys is sometimes a difficult job for an umpire. Once in a while he will go by a player's reputation. On occasion he will base his decision upon instinct. Working a Giant-Dodger game at Ebbets Field one day, home-plate umpire Tom Gorman was getting roasted by the Brooklyn bench. Finally he had enough and based his eviction on reputation *and* instinct. "Van Cuyk, you're through for the day," he said as he charged the Dodger dugout. "Get out of here."

No one on the bench moved.

"Come on, (Chris) Van Cuyk, get moving. Go take a shower."

Still, there was no movement. Gorman then angrily turned toward manager Chuck Dressen and said, "You better get him out of here. If you don't, I'm going to clear the whole bench."

Dressen got the last laugh that time, though. "If you want to thumb Van Cuyk, you'll have to go to St. Paul, 'cause that's where I sent him yesterday."

A Hot, Dry Day

Pitcher Jerry Reuss is a player who likes to have a few laughs around the ball park. At some one else's expense, of course.

For example, one day in Los Angeles the temperature was in the high nineties and Frank Pulli, who was working the plate, was desperately looking forward to a cold drink. Reuss, feeling sorry for Pulli, sent the ball boy out with a drink for the umpire in between innings. Appreciatively, Pulli accepted it and proceeded to down a lusty gulp of *hot coffee.*

Dust in the Eye

Sometimes a manager has to make a quick pitching move, and the relief pitcher doesn't have enough time to warm up properly. That was the case when manager Charlie Dressen of the Dodgers hurriedly rushed Clyde King into a game at Ebbets Field. After his preliminary warm-up throws, King simply wasn't ready to pitch.

So shortstop Pee Wee Reese, the team's captain, went into his patented stalling act. He called time out and told the umpires he had a speck of dust in his eye. Then he walked over to third baseman Billy Cox, who proceeded to become a partner in Reese's deceit.

In the meantime, King was supposed to be taking advantage of Reese's ruse by making additional warm-up throws. He became so fascinated with Reese's act, however, that he discontinued his warm-up throws, left the mound, and walked over to third base to see what kind of success Cox was having in removing the speck of dust from Pee Wee's eye.

Safe or Out?

In a Phillie-Dodger game one evening umpire Beans Reardon got his messages mixed up. Richie Ashburn came sliding into Brooklyn third baseman Billy Cox, and Reardon shouted safe but signaled out.

"Well, what am I?" Ashburn asked the "caught-on-the-horns-of-a-dilemma" umpire.

"You heard me say safe," Reardon said. "But thirty thousand people saw me signal out. You're outnumbered. Get out of here."

Sound Rulings

Umpire Larry Goetz got burned on a "phantom catch" at first base one day. With a runner on second base, Johnny Moore of the Phillies was the batter, and Sam Leslie of the Giants was the first baseman. Moore hit to the shortstop and ran to first base. In the meantime, Goetz watched for the runner's foot to touch the first-base bag. When Moore was two steps from the bag, however, Leslie slapped his glove with his bare hand, and Goetz made the "Out" call.

Moore, who rarely argued with umpires, charged Goetz on this occasion. Goetz, surprised and curious, decided to listen closely to the player's objection.

"Larry, I've got a solid gripe," Moore said. "Leslie doesn't even have the ball. They didn't even make the play at first. They made it at third."

Bill Terry, the first baseman for the Giants, was one of the best executioners of the "phantom catch." He was a master at stealing an umpire's call.

In the 1933 World Series he took two clear-cut hits away from the Washington Senators because he knew the habits of the first-base umpire, who watched the runner's foot instead of the fielder's glove. Twice in that series Terry slapped his glove with his bare hand, and twice he got the call from the umpire, who let the sound of the ball hitting the first baseman's glove dictate his call.

Joker Altrock

Nick Altrock, the third-base coach for the Senators, was an accomplished umpire baiter. One day a couple of calls by umpire Bill McGowan went against Washington, and Altrock explicitly expressed his displeasure with them.

A few innings later a batter fouled a ball into the third-base stands, and McGowan saw a woman being carried out of the park on a stretcher.

"Did the ball hit her?" McGowan asked Altrock.

"No," the coach snidely replied. "You called the last one right, and she fainted."

Stubborn Manager

One day veteran National League umpire Doug Harvey ejected a manager for protesting one of his ball-and-strike calls too passionately. The manager then stood defiantly on home plate and said he wouldn't leave the field. Finally, Harvey told the hitter to get into the batter's box and ordered the pitcher to throw. The hurler hesitated at first, but when he was directed to throw a second time, he hummed a high hard-one close by the manager's head.

"Strike one!" Harvey bellowed.

Before the moundsman's next pitch, the manager had retreated to the safety of his clubhouse.

Sick

Bill Klem, the great umpire, threw Pie Traynor, the great third baseman of the Pirates, out of a game one hot afternoon in Pittsburgh. That surprised both fans and players alike. Traynor was considered to be an umpire's ballplayer.

"What did he say?" the reporters wanted to know after the game.

"He wasn't feeling well," Klem said.

"We didn't know he was ill."

"Well, that's what he said. He told me he was sick of my stupid decisions."

No Use Sliding

One night when Red Schoendienst was managing the Cardinals, he became incensed when umpire Frank Secory called Mike Shannon out on a play at the plate. In trying to prove that Shannon was safe, Schoendienst demonstrated by sliding into home plate himself.

Secory fired his right hand into the air. "Same as Shannon," he said, "you're out, too. Out of the game."

Maglie the Barber

Today you hear a lot of pitchers complaining because umpires won't let them throw "inside" to the hitter. That wasn't the case in the old days, though.

Some players said that Sal "The Barber" Maglie of the Giants would knock down his own mother on Mother's Day. "I would," he said, "if she was crowding the plate."

Maglie wasn't a loner, but he didn't like to hang out with other players, either. Why? "I don't want to get to know them," he said. "I might get to like them. Then if the occasion arises, I might not want to throw at them."

"Umpire, Help Me!"

Umpires have been accused of virtually everything from favoring one team over another to trying to end games early. But first baseman George "Catfish" Metkovich of the 1952 Pirates may have been the only player who accused an arbiter of failing to help him play his position.

From the first pitch of a game one hot and sultry afternoon in Pittsburgh, Brooklyn Dodger batters were rifling base hits past Metkovich's head and richocheting them off his body. Finally after Duke Snider banked a hard shot off his shins, Metkovich looked at first-base umpire Augie Donatelli and said exasperatingly, "For crying out loud, Augie, don't just stand there. Get a glove and give me a hand."

Eight-Inning Game?

Some players lose track of the number of innings in a game. Take Jim Corsi of the 1989 Oakland A's, for example. Brought up from Tacoma just before a game with the New York Yankees, he was understandably excited. So when Rick Honeycutt of the A's got the final out of the eighth inning, Corsi was the first Oakland player out of the dugout to congratulate the relief pitcher on his *victory*. Also the *only* one.

Honeycutt, who was both confused and amused, looked at the rookie and said, "They play only eight innings at Tacoma?"

An inning later, Honeycutt got the final out of the *game*.

Marvelous Marv

One day "Marvelous" Marv Throneberry of the New York Mets hit an apparent triple, but the opposing team said that the runner missed second base, and they successfully appealed the play. Casey Stengel, manager of the Mets, ran out onto the field to protest the call, but he was stopped by his first-base coach. "Forget it, Casey," the coach said, "he missed first base, too."

Not Al Kaline

Ron Luciano, the former American League umpire, liked to talk to the players. One player he was unsuccessful in talking to was right fielder Al Kaline of the Detroit Tigers.

At the end of a Tiger inning, Kaline would grab his glove and trot out to his position. Luciano, who would be working first base that day, would say, "Hi, Al, how's the family?" Kaline wouldn't respond. Nothing.

That's the way it went for ten years. Then one day, out of the blue, Kaline ran past the umpire and said, "Hi, Ron, how's it going?"

Luciano, who was startled, ran after Kaline, demanding, "Why are you talking to me now? I've been trying to get you to say something for ten years, and you gave me nothing. Why now?"

Kaline replied in a calm and easy voice, "I just wanted to make sure you were going to hang around, Ron."

Pitcher's Notes

Many pitchers have been suspected of doctoring the baseball, and some of them have, in fact, been searched for evidence of the foreign substance. Don Sutton was one of them. But he didn't mind. As a matter of fact, he enjoyed the search, but eluded the seizure. When the umpires searched him, they found numerous notes that he had placed in his pockets: "cold," "colder," "freezing," "warm," "hot," "hotter," and "no trespassing."

Index